Simone Weil: A Very Short Introduction

VERY SHORT INTRODUCTIONS are for anyone wanting a stimulating and accessible way into a new subject. They are written by experts, and have been translated into more than 45 different languages.

The series began in 1995, and now covers a wide variety of topics in every discipline. The VSI library currently contains over 750 volumes—a Very Short Introduction to everything from Psychology and Philosophy of Science to American History and Relativity—and continues to grow in every subject area.

Very Short Introductions available now:

ABOLITIONISM Richard S. Newman
THE ABRAHAMIC RELIGIONS
  Charles L. Cohen
ACCOUNTING Christopher Nobes
ADDICTION Keith Humphreys
ADOLESCENCE Peter K. Smith
THEODOR W. ADORNO
  Andrew Bowie
ADVERTISING Winston Fletcher
AERIAL WARFARE Frank Ledwidge
AESTHETICS Bence Nanay
AFRICAN AMERICAN HISTORY
  Jonathan Scott Holloway
AFRICAN AMERICAN RELIGION
  Eddie S. Glaude Jr.
AFRICAN HISTORY John Parker and
  Richard Rathbone
AFRICAN POLITICS Ian Taylor
AFRICAN RELIGIONS
  Jacob K. Olupona
AGEING Nancy A. Pachana
AGNOSTICISM Robin Le Poidevin
AGRICULTURE Paul Brassley and
  Richard Soffe
ALEXANDER THE GREAT
  Hugh Bowden
ALGEBRA Peter M. Higgins
AMERICAN BUSINESS HISTORY
  Walter A. Friedman
AMERICAN CULTURAL HISTORY
  Eric Avila
AMERICAN FOREIGN RELATIONS
  Andrew Preston
AMERICAN HISTORY Paul S. Boyer

AMERICAN IMMIGRATION
  David A. Gerber
AMERICAN INTELLECTUAL
  HISTORY
  Jennifer Ratner-Rosenhagen
THE AMERICAN JUDICIAL SYSTEM
  Charles L. Zelden
AMERICAN LEGAL HISTORY
  G. Edward White
AMERICAN MILITARY HISTORY
  Joseph T. Glatthaar
AMERICAN NAVAL HISTORY
  Craig L. Symonds
AMERICAN POETRY David Caplan
AMERICAN POLITICAL HISTORY
  Donald Critchlow
AMERICAN POLITICAL PARTIES
  AND ELECTIONS L. Sandy Maisel
AMERICAN POLITICS
  Richard M. Valelly
THE AMERICAN PRESIDENCY
  Charles O. Jones
THE AMERICAN REVOLUTION
  Robert J. Allison
AMERICAN SLAVERY
  Heather Andrea Williams
THE AMERICAN SOUTH
  Charles Reagan Wilson
THE AMERICAN WEST
  Stephen Aron
AMERICAN WOMEN'S HISTORY
  Susan Ware
AMPHIBIANS T. S. Kemp
ANAESTHESIA Aidan O'Donnell

VOLTAIRE Nicholas Cronk
WAR AND RELIGION Jolyon Mitchell
    and Joshua Rey
WAR AND TECHNOLOGY Alex Roland
WATER John Finney
WAVES Mike Goldsmith
WEATHER Storm Dunlop
SIMONE WEIL A. Rebecca Rozelle-Stone
THE WELFARE STATE David Garland
WITCHCRAFT Malcolm Gaskill
WITTGENSTEIN A. C. Grayling

WORK Stephen Fineman
WORLD MUSIC Philip Bohlman
WORLD MYTHOLOGY David Leeming
THE WORLD TRADE
    ORGANIZATION
    Amrita Narlikar
WORLD WAR II Gerhard L. Weinberg
WRITING AND SCRIPT
    Andrew Robinson
ZIONISM Michael Stanislawski
ÉMILE ZOLA Brian Nelson

Available soon:

DOSTOEVSKY Deborah Martinsen
THUCYDIDES Jennifer T. Roberts

BRITISH ARCHITECTURE Dana Arnold
SUSTAINABILITY Saleem H. Ali

For more information visit our website

www.oup.com/vsi/

A. Rebecca Rozelle-Stone

SIMONE WEIL

A Very Short Introduction

Great Clarendon Street, Oxford, OX2 6DP,
United Kingdom

Oxford University Press is a department of the University of Oxford.
It furthers the University's objective of excellence in research, scholarship,
and education by publishing worldwide. Oxford is a registered trade mark of
Oxford University Press in the UK and in certain other countries

Published in the United States of America by Oxford University Press
198 Madison Avenue, New York, NY 10016, United States of America

British Library Cataloguing in Publication Data
Data available

Library of Congress Control Number: 2023942607

ISBN 978–0–19–284696–9

Printed by Integrated Books International, United States of America

To Lucian,
the most attentive person I know

Contents

Acknowledgements

This volume would not be possible without the support of certain
, persons and organizations.

First, I am indebted to Lucian W. Stone, my partner in life and
reader/first editor of all my writing. I am beyond grateful for the
time, care, and attention you have given to all of my drafts, as well
as the encouragement you constantly provide before, during, and
after the extended process of writing.

I am so thankful for the friendships, originating in a shared
interest in Simone Weil, which have sustained me in the last
several years. The support, enlightening conversations, and
inspirations provided by Mariëtte Willemsen and her incredible
Weil seminar students at Amsterdam University College; Antonio
Calcagno; and Diane Enns have been invaluable in restoring my
energies when the world at large is fatiguing.

I am also appreciative for the generosity of Sylvie Weil, niece of
Simone Weil and fellow writer herself, who graciously provided
the photographs of her late aunt, along with their permissions.
This work would not be complete without those crucial inclusions.

I owe my gratitude to the superbly helpful editors at Oxford
University Press—particularly Latha Menon and Imogene

Haslam—who provided me with astute and discerning suggestions to improve my writing and bring greater clarity to Weil's ideas.

Thank you to the University of North Dakota and especially its College of Arts and Sciences, which has supported my research and writing on Simone Weil for well over a decade.

I am grateful for the members of the American Weil Society, many of whom have been excellent interlocutors with me over the years, providing essential feedback on my work, including: Eric O. Springsted, Benjamin P. Davis, Sophie Bourgault, Lissa McCullough, Inese Radzins, Scott Ritner, Beatrice Marovich, Mario von der Ruhr, and Lawrence Schmidt.

Finally, I wish to thank my dear parents, Hal and Ava Rozelle, for their incredible patience with and support of me over the months of my writing.

List of illustrations

Note: All photographs of Simone Weil have been generously provided by Sylvie Weil and are printed here with her permission. Other photographs are public domain.

Simone Weil

Abbreviations

References in the text to Simone Weil's writings are given by an abbreviation of the title, followed by a page reference.

LPW	*Simone Weil: Late Philosophical Writings*, trans. Eric O. Springsted and Lawrence E. Schmidt (Notre Dame, Ind.: Notre Dame University Press, 2015).
N	*The Notebooks of Simone Weil*, trans. Arthur Wills (London: Routledge, 2004).
NR	*The Need for Roots*, trans. Arthur Wills (London: Routledge, 2002).
OL	*Oppression and Liberty*, trans. Arthur Wills and John Petrie (Amherst, Mass.: University of Massachusetts Press, 1973).
SE	*Selected Essays 1934–43*, ed. and trans. Richard Rees (Eugene, Ore.: Wipf & Stock, 2015).
SL	*Seventy Letters*, trans. Richard Rees (London: Oxford University Press, 1965).
SNL	*On Science, Necessity, and the Love of God*, trans. Richard Rees (London: Oxford University Press, 1968).
WG	*Waiting for God*, trans. Emma Craufurd (New York: Perennial Classics, 2001).

Chapter 1
A life and death of attention

To tell the story of Simone Weil is not an easy task, in part because
the exacting moral and spiritual demands she placed on herself
would put any admiring scholar of hers to shame. To think about
her life and to read her thoughts can feel like an indictment. But
Weil was also a thinker who eschewed attention to her person,
insisting that the only things that matter are the ideas themselves.
She strived to attain impersonal, eternal truths in her living and
writing, and she saw the interest in her personal characteristics or
idiosyncrasies as a superficial distraction—a way to avoid the
essential. In one of her last letters to her parents, just a few weeks
before she died, Weil compared herself to the Shakespearean fools
who, she believed, represented the only class of people—those who
are humiliated, impoverished, exiled from social consideration—
that are able to tell the truth. Because of their lowly social station,
however, they are ridiculed and never listened to. Weil recognized
that her prestigious education might appear to separate her from
this category, but she believed that the acclaim for her intelligence
was 'positively *intended* to evade the question: "Is what she says
true?"' (SL 201).

To be fixated on the person is perhaps to miss the point of this
philosopher, who much preferred the self-effacing label of 'fool' to
the high regard for her intellect by the end of her life. Yet for those
of us who seek to understand the ideas she sought to convey and

to ascertain whether they might in fact be true, it is difficult, if not impossible, to grasp the full measure and substance of those ideas without discerning their embodiment in her unique life.

The relatively short but striking life of French philosopher Simone Weil began on 3 February 1909, in Paris, France. She was the second child of Bernard Weil and Selma Reinherz, upper-middle-class secular Jewish parents who were highly cultured and passed on to their children a love of learning and disregard for materialistic and frivolous concerns. Her familial-cultural context was one of religious agnosticism but informed by a combination of classical Greek and secularized Judaeo-Christian values. There are several anecdotes about Simone and her older brother André (who would go on to become a famous mathematician) which reveal the extent of the children's highly intelligent and precocious temperaments. For instance, when André and Simone were very young, André received a children's book about the ancient Greeks and Romans. One day, when little Simone was alone in her crib, she was given the book to occupy her with its pictures; shortly thereafter, her parents heard her say, 'Is it true that Romans exist? I am afraid of the Romans!' Roughly 30 years later, she would write about the evil of the ancient Romans in her notebooks, describing how they epitomized brute force and the evil of empire.

Indeed, this sensitivity to suffering and repulsion by violence and injustice seemingly characterized Weil her entire life, as did a strong disdain for the excesses of bourgeois life in general (represented to some extent by her parents) and feminine adornments in particular. One of Weil's cousins visited her when she was barely 3 years old and gave her a ring set complete with a large jewel. Weil reportedly said, 'I do not like luxury', which made her entire family laugh and became the basis for a long-standing family joke.

In 1915, the family moved to Mayenne, France, due to a new job assignment for Bernard, who was a doctor. It was there, when

Simone was 5 years old, that she and André began corresponding with French soldiers fighting at the front who had no living families and who had to survive on tight rations, adopting them as 'godsons' and sending them most of their sugar and all of their chocolate. Simone had even insisted on working for one particular adopted soldier, gathering wood and tying it into small bundles, for which she would receive compensation from her parents, which was then spent on care packages for him. Weeks later, this soldier would visit the Weils in person when he was on leave, and he would take walks with Simone each day. Shortly after his visit, he was killed in action.

Such a committed response to the plight of the war-weary was typical for Weil, who seemed to feel guilty and be hyper-conscious of her own family's privilege in the face of broader human misery and misfortune. Throughout her life, her approach to this disequilibrium usually consisted of some form of self-denial of what the others could not enjoy or deliberately taking up work or other activities that were a necessity for the working classes, as a means of identifying with some of the most oppressed and exploited groups in her society. Always concerned about the situation of the poor and disenfranchised, when she was 11, Weil joined workers who were on strike on the Boulevard Saint Michel below her family's apartment, chanting the Internationale.

Undoubtedly, such actions and sympathies must have been troubling for Bernard and Selma, who had worked to provide comfortable lives for their children and who felt that suffering was something to be reduced or eliminated through science and familial support. It was not unusual for her parents to intervene when Weil's attempts at solidarity resulted in accident or her own bodily harm, as when she accidentally and badly burned herself with a pot of boiling oil soon after she had attempted to join the Spanish Civil War. She was retrieved from a field hospital by her parents, who were surely at a loss to understand their daughter's absurd determinations.

Simone and André Weil

Weil also admired her brother very much and wanted to reflect his intellectual virtues and stoic attitude. There were apparently few toys in their house except for a ball, and the children primarily engaged in intellectual games and contests within a literary universe they cultivated for themselves. They would recite whole scenes from Corneille and Racine; Simone would spend a good deal of time in thought, even as a child. It was André who taught Simone to read the newspaper when she was 6, and he also modelled for her a serious preoccupation with education, particularly in classical science and mathematics. When staying at Ballaigues in Switzerland, the two children would spend many days in large open fields going on what they called 'exploratory journeys'. They would pick flowers and catch butterflies, but of course, they would release the latter, out of sympathy for all forms of wildlife.

Simone and André were inseparable when they were young (Figure 1), and Weil idolized her brother's intelligence, in contrast to the frivolous and superficial concerns expected of young women. She mostly rejected feminine attire and expectations, resenting a comment made by a visitor to her mother who had declared of Simone and André that the latter was 'genius itself', while Simone was the 'beauty'. Thereafter, Weil did her best to downplay any manifestation of femininity in her appearance and avoid social charms expected of French women in the early 20th century. When she was young, she never played with dolls and did not want to sew, and when she was older, she dressed in baggy, oversized clothing that would not draw attention to her body. As a child, she reportedly remarked, 'It would be better if everyone was dressed in the same way and for a *sou*. That way people could work and no differences would be apparent among them.'

While she later actively disavowed the label of 'feminist' (for this term connoted to her an emphasis on gender-identity struggles

1. André and his sister, Simone Weil, vacationing in Belgium, summer 1922.

that she saw as peripheral to the concerns about widespread, impersonal suffering), it seems clear that Weil was deliberately resisting the patriarchal and sexist imperatives of her time, in her own ways. Her mother Selma was also an influence, calling Simone 'our son number two' or 'Simon' and intentionally trying to cultivate in her daughter a strength of intellect and forthrightness that was typically reserved for and attributed to men. Later on, Weil's niece (André's daughter) Sylvie would describe in her book, *At Home with André and Simone Weil*, how she found it impossible to believe that Simone had ever wept: 'This person whom my father always depicted as strong and derisive, could she cry? The double of my father, this macho double, really wept? I could not imagine it. I never really saw her as a female.'

Simone remained close to André until the end of her life, celebrating his marriage to Eveline and adoring little Sylvie. In the spring of 1940, André had been charged for failure to report for military duty, having previously committed to being a conscientious objector; he was sentenced to five years in prison. He served time in Rouen, France, and was frequently visited by Simone and their family. He and Simone would argue about Nietzsche in ancient Greek—André loved him while Simone detested him. She would also tease André about his landing in jail before her, although she blamed herself for his uncompromising pacifist stance. In the winter of 1940, André's sentence would be commuted, and a year later, he would arrive in the United States, ahead of his parents and sister.

One of Weil's last letters to André was dated 17 April 1943. In it, she shared more about her growing physical fatigue and weakness than she would admit to their parents, and she asked him not to divulge these facts, not wanting to worry them about her worsening condition.

Health issues and concerns with purity

Throughout her life, Weil was notably averse to being touched or kissed, even by her family, and she felt uncomfortable with explicit displays of affection. She also did not like to eat or touch certain things, especially those items that had been handled by others. Some of these aversions were probably induced by the influence of Bernard's job as a physician, the family's friendship with the famous bacteriologist Élie Metchnikov, and Selma's obsession with hygiene, cleanliness, and avoidance of disease. Selma did not want people to kiss her children, and she taught André and Simone to be fastidious about washing their hands and avoiding contagion. When Metchnikov once attempted to kiss Simone's hand, she began to cry, 'Water! Water!' and ran away to wash herself.

This kind of concern for cleanliness and purity is arguably manifest in Weil's later social, moral, and, eventually, religious convictions, as well as in her oft-cited feelings of disgust which were frequently directed towards herself for her own perceived selfishness or failures. Could it be that this overarching tendency towards moral purity was a factor in her death at the early age of 34? Indeed, her writings reveal an uncompromising thinker who viewed her own existence and self as a stain on the beauty of the world, so that her vocation must centre on continual self-renunciation and self-displacement.

Weil's precarious health was also an issue throughout her life. When she was only 3, she suffered a violent attack of appendicitis, which was initially misdiagnosed. At this time, operations weren't performed immediately, so little Simone stayed in the hospital in Auteuil for three weeks due to other complications, and she would talk while under chloroform. Interestingly, while observing her in this state and during her convalescence, Weil's physician, Dr Goldmann, told Selma that he didn't think Simone would survive, as it seemed to him that such a young child capable of saying the things she did was too extraordinary to go on living.

When she was 12, Weil began experiencing the severe and chronic migraine headaches that would go on to plague her for the rest of her life. These violent headaches also made eating more challenging, as chewing food exacerbated her pain and induced nausea. The headaches would become more intense through the years, at times nearly paralysing her or making work impossible. At 14 years old, Weil fell into a deep depression and considered taking her own life. This adolescent crisis was at least partially spurred by her sense of intellectual inadequacy in comparison with her brother's evident mathematical genius, which she likened to that of Blaise Pascal; meanwhile, Weil believed she was academically mediocre. The intensity of the headaches also gave her a feeling of general unworthiness and seemed to be an outward manifestation of her inward misery. She later wrote: 'I didn't mind having no visible successes, but what did grieve me was the idea of being excluded from that transcendent kingdom to which only the truly great have access and wherein truth abides. I preferred to die rather than live without that truth' (WG 23).

Fortunately, Weil recovered from this deep despair, even though her sense of inadequacy and mediocrity never really left her. She developed an idea of the salvific effects of *desiring* truth and goodness, suggesting that anyone who desires and makes sincere efforts to attain truth, beauty, and virtue can pierce into the realm of truth reserved for genius: 'The conviction that had come to me was that when one hungers for bread, one does not receive stones' (WG 24).

Education and philosophical influences

Simone Weil desperately desired to increase her knowledge and understanding of the world, and this orientation was evident throughout her formal education, as well as through her writings and gestures of solidarity with the most exploited classes of society. In 1924, she was admitted to the baccalaureate in Classics at the Lycée Victor Duruy, unsure of whether to specialize in mathematics or philosophy, but eventually settling on the latter. She apparently fitted the stereotype of a philosophy student, not caring about her appearance and walking around deep in thought with ink-stained clothes. She was rather introverted, and her fellow students found her intimidating. One of her teachers at Duruy was the famous philosopher René Le Senne; he confirmed that she was one of the best students he had ever encountered, and his professed philosophical idealism undoubtedly impacted the evolution of her thought.

In 1925, Weil earned her baccalaureate in philosophy, allowing her to transfer to Lycée Henri IV so that she could prepare for her university entrance exam to the prestigious École Normale Supérieure (ENS). Henri IV had just begun admitting female students, and Weil was one of only three women (the other two being Simone Pétrement, Weil's eventual biographer, and Lucienne Cervières) in a class of 30 when she entered the school.

It was at Henri IV that she met the prominent philosopher-teacher known as 'Alain'—Émile-Auguste Chartier—who would become a major influence on Weil's philosophical interests and development. Alain gave his students a solid background in the history of Western philosophy, emphasizing idealists and rationalists like Plato, Descartes, Spinoza, and Kant, as well as lessons from his own teacher, Jules Lagneau, a noted reader of Kantian philosophy. But Alain also introduced Weil and other students to great works of literature, particularly those of Homer, Greek tragedians like Aeschylus, Sophocles, and Euripides, stoics like Marcus Aurelius, and French writers like Voltaire and Balzac.

Alain lectured on a wide range of ideas that seemingly inspired Weil, including: the centrality of the human will in moral life; the meaning of attention; the link between genius and purity in art; and the importance of labour in revealing us to ourselves. Alain was also a formative influence on her writing practice and style, helping her to cultivate a disciplined practice of writing down her thoughts and questions in journals, as well as suggesting exercises to his students designed to focus the attention around a single topic for extensive exploration through essay, called *topos*. He was convinced that learning to write well would result in learning to think well, and he believed that writing is more honest than speaking because 'it does not have to take account of the listeners'. Alain was trying to teach his students to express fundamental truths in clear and precise language—a skill that Weil exemplified in her terse but powerful notebook aphorisms and philosophical meditations, in her letters, and in her more formal essays.

It was during this time, when Weil was preparing for the exam to enter ENS as well as for the four certificates that would constitute her licence to teach philosophy, that she met the soon-to-be famous existentialist-feminist philosopher Simone de Beauvoir at

the Sorbonne, where both were studying and taking the
certification exams. In her *Memoirs of a Dutiful Daughter*
Beauvoir recalled:

> [Weil] intrigued me because of her great reputation for intelligence
> and her bizarre outfit; she would stroll around in the courtyard of
> the Sorbonne attended by a group of Alain's old students...A great
> famine had broken out in China, and I was told that when she
> heard the news she had wept: these tears compelled my respect
> much more than her gifts as a philosopher. I envied her for having a
> heart that could beat right across the world.

Beauvoir noted that on one occasion, she managed to strike up a
conversation with Weil, who promptly declared that only one
thing mattered in the world: 'the Revolution that would feed all
the starving people on the earth'. Beauvoir in turn replied that 'the
problem was not to make men happy, but to find the reason for
their existence'. Upon hearing this, Weil had looked Beauvoir up
and down and retorted: '"It's easy to see that you've never gone
hungry."' Their interactions ended there, for Beauvoir was
annoyed that Weil had apparently labelled and dismissed her as
an out-of-touch bourgeoise. By the summer of 1927, Weil had
earned all four of the teaching certificates; Beauvoir reported that
Weil was at the very top of the list of candidates who had earned
the certificate in 'General Philosophy and Logic'.

At Henri IV, Weil was already a principled rebel and troublemaker
for school officials, something she seemed to take pride in and
understand as a sign of loyalty to Alain. One administrator had
decided that men and women should sit in separate areas, so Weil
had determined to make this absurdity explicit by preparing two
cards with inscriptions reading 'Men's side' and 'Women's side',
respectively. As she was putting them up, the official caught her
and tried to snatch them from her, whereupon they came to blows.
In the same year, she was suspended for eight days for smoking in
the men's courtyard; the problem was that all the courtyards were

for men. The school principal ultimately approached her in the Luxembourg Gardens and chastised her for her 'bad conduct: unimaginable attire, masculine actions, nonconformity'.

But in Alain, Weil had an ally and supporter. He had indicated that the administration was one of those powers which a free person obeys with a certain detachment, but without trusting it too much. He could perceive the depth of substance and extraordinary potential in Weil, beyond her baggy attire, idiosyncrasies, social awkwardness, and incessant smoking. According to Marie-Magdeleine Davy, an acquaintance and eventual biographer of Weil, Alain thought Simone to be 'superior, and by a great margin, to all the others of her generation'.

Teaching and activist work

From 1928 to 1931 Weil studied at the ENS. She was the only woman in her class, the first woman having been admitted in 1917. She wrote her dissertation on knowledge and perception in the philosophy of Descartes, and in 1931, she attained her *agrégation* in philosophy at the age of 22. After receiving her diploma, she served from late 1931 to mid-1934 as a teacher at various *lycées*. Throughout this period, outside of her teaching duties at each school, Weil also taught philosophy to, lobbied for, and wrote on behalf of workers' groups; at times, moreover, she herself engaged in manual labour.

Her first teaching post was at an all-girls' school in Le Puy-en-Vélay, a small conservative town in the south of France. She taught philosophy and literature, but she didn't use prescribed textbooks or follow a specific curriculum. Taking a cue from Alain, Weil developed her own unique pedagogy using primary works she selected, and she had her students write a lot, reflecting on the ideas of philosophers she had studied extensively: Plato, Descartes, Kant, Aurelius, and Marx, among others. She was trying to develop the capacity for deep attention in her students, and she was less concerned about whether they were prepared to pass the examinations.

In her spare time, Weil engaged in actions that revealed her own philosophy and attentiveness to those who were marginalized or exploited in her country. For instance, she would travel to Saint-Étienne to discuss (with Albertine Thévenon, the assistant secretary of the trade union movement there) how the unions could improve the lives and conditions of the workers, especially if the latter did not fully understand the syndicalist/union movement. She developed a workers' university there. She also gave away significant portions of her own income to workers so that they could purchase books for their classes. She began offering lectures on French and Political Economy at the office of the Labour Exchange, and she would go down mine shafts and work a pneumatic drill to try to connect with the unique experiences of the miners, who came to admire her. Given her preceding reputation as an activist and troublemaker, Weil was surveilled from the time she arrived in Le Puy, and some parents were beginning to take notice of her radical methods and activities. Despite student petitions and union support, she was eventually transferred to Auxerre in late 1932.

However, before transferring to Auxerre, Weil travelled to Germany to learn about the growing fascist movement there. She was impressed by the culture of the German working classes and found that the German trade unions were the site of the greatest potential for generating a revolution, but unfortunately, they were merely reformist in nature. Plus, she noted that extensive periods of unemployment had left the German people generally devoid of energy and motivation to effectively resist the fascist momentum. She was also disappointed in the German Communist Party, given the great disjunct between its own political rhetoric and its actions; the workers who had been the base of the party had succumbed to fatigue, inertia, and passivity, and the party itself had become an example of the worst type of bureaucratic machinery. The Communists did not appear to understand the growing threat of Nazism, and they did not demonstrate real support for the working classes. The experience was overwhelming for Weil; when she returned home from Germany, she wept.

While at Le Puy, Weil had refused any conveniences for herself that might have been labelled 'luxury', and she continually sought ways to be in solidarity with those who were not as fortunate as her. In addition to giving away most of her salary to welfare funds, assistance agencies, and the Solidarity Fund of the miners of Saint-Étienne, she also refused rugs and heaters for her room, jewellery and fine clothes, decorative wallpaper, and various kinds of food deemed too extravagant. At all times she wished to cross over class lines and to share the results of her study with workers, as much as with her actual students. This orientation persisted at Auxerre and then at Roanne, her next two teaching posts.

At Auxerre, despite the fact that her students loved her and had even helped her type materials for railway workers, because only a small percentage of them passed the final exams in philosophy (as at Le Puy), school officials decided to abolish the Chair of Philosophy. Weil was therefore dismissed in June 1933. Her next teaching assignment was at Roanne (Figure 2), but here, too, she was alienated from her colleagues, largely because of her political views, her actions on behalf of workers, and her peculiar mannerisms. One fellow teacher at Roanne noted that Weil was a stranger among them, even at mealtime, reporting that it frequently seemed Weil was not really present in the communal table conversations; she 'would read Karl Marx directly from the original text and continue to eat'.

During the Christmas holidays of 1933, Weil went home to spend time with her parents in Paris. While there, she persuaded them to host Leon Trotsky, who was in France for a meeting with friends and in search of an appropriate venue. Weil was eager to converse

2. Simone Weil with her students at the Lycée des Jeunes Filles, along with the director, at Roanne.

with Trotsky, but their meeting ended up exasperating them both, as they disagreed on almost everything. She became more disenchanted with political parties and politicians, while her interest in sharing the experiences of ordinary workers increased.

The following year (1934), Weil requested and received a year of unpaid leave from her teaching post to gain first-hand experience of factory work, beginning with the Alsthom factory in Paris. Her primary goal was to fully understand the relationship between humans and the world, or between culture and modern technology, via engagement with industrial work that, she thought, would help to clarify certain gaps between theory and action. Her factory experiences and the important insights she gleaned from them will be detailed at length in Chapter 3, but suffice it to say, she learned that factories produced a degrading sense of humiliation and paralysis of thought in their workers, tantamount to a kind of slavery. She lasted a little less than a year in the factories due to her fragile health.

Following her difficult time in the factories, in 1935 Weil accompanied her parents on a trip to Portugal, where she had the first of three intensely religious experiences, all Christian in nature.

By the summer of 1936, Weil's attention turned to the Spanish Civil War. With a revolutionary hope, an inability to remain passively watching from afar, and sympathy for the Spanish anarchists, she set off for Spain to support the Loyalists, while vowing that she would never use the gun that was provided for her (Figure 3). She had been a committed pacifist ever since her school days with Alain. But given her experiences with the growing fascist movement in Germany and her newfound understanding of the dehumanization of people in factories, she began to wrestle with the question: 'Do we or do we not want to look matters in the face, to set the problem of war or peace in its entirety?' But while the struggle in Spain was coming to a close,

Simone Weil

3. Simone Weil in her Federación Anarquista uniform on her return from the Spanish Civil War front, 1936.

Weil endured quite the anticlimactic accident: she mistakenly stepped into a pot of boiling cooking oil, badly injuring herself and requiring her parents to rescue her from a field hospital.

This clumsy accident did not stop Weil from desiring political, or even wartime, involvement. When Hitler invaded Prague and after the military alliance between Germany and Italy, Weil renounced her pacifist beliefs but was forced to flee Paris with her parents, seeking temporary respite in Marseilles in June 1940. There, she engaged in political efforts like distributing anti-fascist and anti-Nazi literature and visiting prison camps. She also began devising (rather impractical) plans to establish a corps of nurses who would be parachuted into the front lines of war in France to care for the wounded fighters of the Resistance—plans which were, of course, never realized. Having learned about her 'nurses project', Charles de Gaulle had apparently exclaimed, 'But she is mad!' This rejection was a major blow to Weil. News of Germany's occupation of the Free Zone made her feel guilty about ever leaving France.

Weil did, however, seek out and find agricultural work on a farm during this time, spending eight hours a day in a vineyard picking grapes, even in the rain. She also reportedly carried a copy of Plato's *Symposium* around and, true to her interest in worker education, attempted to teach the text to fellow labourers. The farm belonged to Gustave Thibon, a Catholic writer-philosopher, who was introduced to Weil by the Dominican priest and her spiritual interlocutor Joseph-Marie Perrin. Even though she knew Thibon for a relatively short time, Weil became close to him from working the harvest, and in 1942, she gave him her *Cahiers* (*Notebooks*) for safe keeping. A few years later, Thibon would select many passages from the *Notebooks*, organize them thematically, and publish these selections under the title *La Pesanteur et la grâce* (*Gravity and Grace*). Later, in summer 1942, motivated by a desire to get her parents to safety, she left Marseilles with them to eventually settle in New York.

In New York, Weil was still intent upon getting back to Europe to join the Resistance. She sought meaningful and dangerous work, as she believed that only a sufficiently difficult post and high level of physical investment would relieve her of the despair stemming from her distance from the action and the impotence she felt in the face of so much suffering around the world. She specifically desired to join the Free French movement in London, and at the end of the year, she at last departed New York for London (Figure 4). Her work in London was not what she had hoped. She was appointed editor in the civilian department, where she analysed committee reports from the Free Zone and drew up proposals for the particulars of a French constitution, as well as suggestions for the legal, administrative, and educational principles of a post-war France. The ideas stemming from this work were later published in *L'Enracinement* (*The Need for Roots*).

4. Simone Weil's France Combattante ID pass from war-torn France, when she took refuge in London with her family, March 1943, about five months before she died.

Dying attending

Simone Weil's revolutionary work in schools, factories, mines, fields, and beyond was always characterized by attention, as was, arguably, her death. Although the manner of her death may have been consistent with the values evinced in her life, it still came as a shock to those who knew her. Her former teacher Alain, still in France, kept repeating, 'She will come back surely,' and 'It isn't true!' (WG xviii). She had never been particularly healthy, given her extreme headaches and the meagre amounts of food she would allow herself. Once she arrived in England, her health began to deteriorate more rapidly. In April of 1943, she was diagnosed with pulmonary tuberculosis.

While her initial prognosis was hopeful, Weil was not the ideal patient: she did not comply with the doctors' orders to rest and eat sufficiently. Attentive to the fact that her countrymen and countrywomen had to live off minimal food rations under German occupation, Weil would not allow herself to eat any more than what she believed they were permitted. (It is likely that she exaggerated the dietary restrictions of the French people.) Exhausted, dreadfully thin, feverish, and severely weakened by her fasting and complications with tuberculosis, on 24 August 1943, Weil died at Grosvenor Sanatorium in Kent, apparently peacefully in her sleep. She had kept her illness from most of her friends and loved ones, including her parents, as she did not want to worry them. Three days after her death, the coroner had pronounced it a suicide—cardiac failure due to self-starvation and tuberculosis. But for those who were familiar with Weil's moral principles and work, her death seems to be entirely consistent with her characteristic self-abnegating gestures of solidarity. It seems more likely, at least to this author, that Weil's death was the logical result of her deep attention to the suffering of others. On 30 August 1943, she was laid to rest at Ashford's New Cemetery, between the Jewish and Catholic sections.

Upon learning about Simone Weil's short and uncompromised existence, you may ask: *But what use is this asceticism? How did her dying at 34 years of age benefit anyone? Of what profit is this kind of self-annihilating life?* And such questions are entirely legitimate. The attentive life as described and exemplified by Weil *is* absurd and is *not* profitable or pragmatic. It consumes you while putting your own consumptive tendencies in check. Being attentive in the Weilian sense, you will likely be considered strange, highly sensitive, masochistic, maladjusted, and people will persistently worry about you. Attending to the world might even be the death of you, as it was for her. But the life of attention is also one lived with clear moral intentionality and an intense, unrelenting passion for justice. Such an orientation produces true words without cliché, compassionate gestures without an ounce of condescending pity, and radically self-demanding ideas with a potential to rectify many recurrent ills of our world.

Chapter 2
Greek inspiration

One of the first things a student of Simone Weil will realize is the extent of the ancient Greek philosophers' influence upon her thought. However, this being the case, the reader may wonder what relevance ancient Greek thought (and by extension, therefore, Weil's philosophy) holds for the issues and questions that insistently present themselves to us currently. Yet in a time of devastating political and environmental crises that are largely due to our attraction to excess, personal greed and wilful ignorance, obsession with appearances and trivial distractions, rejection of facts/reality, oblique and inflammatory political rhetoric, and degraded expressions of justice, I contend that we need a renaissance of ancient Greek inspiration—particularly through Weil's 20th-century lens—more than we realize.

In thinking through the events and atrocities of her day, Weil certainly perceived the urgent but still timeless lessons from writers like Homer, Sophocles, Aeschylus, Pythagoras, and, of course, Plato. Readers should keep in mind that Weil was no mere exegete of their writings; indeed, she often made unorthodox interpretations that fitted with her eclectic influences and unique Christian outlook—such as her claim that 'Plato is an authentic mystic and even the father of Occidental mysticism' (IC 77). Rather than expecting a traditional reading of the works, we should understand that these ancient Greek texts served as rich *inspirations* for many of her core values and theories. Accordingly, this chapter is centred on four important social, political, and ethical themes that emerged from her deep familiarity with and admiration for the ancient Greek tradition, namely the nature of power and balance (or equilibrium); justice (in contradistinction to 'rights'); the relation between contradiction and truth; and desire for the good.

At the outset, I should address the omission of Aristotle from the group of Greek thinkers that were explicitly formative in Weil's philosophical development. This was no accidental omission; in fact, Weil wrote that while Aristotle might be the only philosopher 'in the modern sense' from Greece, nevertheless, 'he is quite outside the Greek tradition' (IC 74). In part, this statement reveals as much about how she understood the Greek tradition as it does her criticism of Aristotle. Weil thought the ancient Greeks—pre-eminently Plato—expressed a profound mysticism wherein the soul can be turned towards and even united with the transcendent good, whereas Aristotle's emphasis on rational deliberation and employment of the will in effecting moral action was at odds with her understanding of how attention to the divine produces goodness, in spite (not because) of an ego-driven will.

Aristotle aside, Weil thought that the ancient Greeks had a particularly incisive grasp of the human condition and misery, given that, in her reading, the origin of their civilization occurred via the destruction of Troy. According to her, they were haunted by the memory of that violent devastation and human destitution, and their remorse (rather than any nationalistic pride) coloured and shaped their collective memory and ongoing values. As a result, she believed that Greek civilization was uniquely interested in 'a search for bridges to relate human misery and divine perfection'—that is, some sort of mediation to connect the suffering and limitations of the temporal order with the grace and absolute Goodness of the eternal order (IC 75). Ancient Greek art, poetry, sciences, geometry, mechanics, and philosophy all represent (attempts at) bridges. But for Weil, such a quest for mediation between the mortal and the immortal, or the finite and the infinite, is also spiritual, by definition. To understand these 'bridges' (which Weil called *metaxu*), however, we must begin with the central notion of balance and how power affects it.

Power and balance

Weil recognized that the idea of equilibrium was at the core of Greek thought as well as that of earlier Egyptian values. This concept is represented by the symbol of the balance, where both sides have equivalent weights. Within the context of human society, analysing social equilibrium necessitates a preliminary understanding of the nature of power. Weil was well aware of the natural mechanisms set off by the presence of power, both within the broader *polis* and within the individual *psyche*. It is important to remember that her descriptions of moral and political phenomena (like the employment of power) are frequently presented as analogous to natural, physical laws. In her *Pre-War Notebook*, reflecting on the character of tyranny, Weil advises that we ought to think of people in power as 'dangerous *things*' whom we must avoid as much as possible without lapsing into cowardice when courage is demanded.

That powerful people are to be considered 'things' reflects Weil's observation that powerful persons' complete self-absorption and their sense of supreme importance and infallibility are likely intractable and are even prone to hubristic expansion. We might think that the psyche of a tyrant is characterized by inner turmoil, but the case is worse: just like the total domination of a people by tyrannical rule, there is also complete suppression of the reasoning, thinking, and attentive faculties by the rapacious, ego-driven energies of the power-hungry so that they have no experience of moral conflict. 'Evil dwells in the heart of the criminal without being felt there,' Weil notes (WG 70). Moreover, what is terrible about power, she continues, is that 'it contains the *unlimited.* It is terrible for the tyrant, whom it makes mad. But it is terrible for the slave also. Is there a stoic in the world who could not be degraded by the simplest cruelties, such as hunger and blows, if he were at the mercy of an absolutely lawless whim?' (FLN 17).

In the background of this description of unlimited power and its sadism we can also see Weil's concept of force, which she beautifully and devastatingly characterized in her famous essay (1939) 'The *Iliad* or the Poem of Force'. Inspired by Homer's well-known epic poem, it is here that Weil depicts force as the protagonist and 'true subject' of the *Iliad,* something that enslaves and degrades both those who employ it and those who are subjected to its violence. Especially with regard to the latter, she defines force as 'that x that turns anybody who is subjected to it into a *thing.* Exercised to the limit, it turns man into a thing in the most literal sense: it makes a corpse out of him' (ANTH 163). There is also, as she notes, force that does not kill (or does not kill *just yet*), but such force is prominently displayed in threats and in torture scenarios. Even here, Weil suggests, force has the uncanny ability to turn a human into a thing while they are still alive:

> A man stands disarmed and naked with a weapon pointing at him; this person becomes a corpse before anybody or anything touches him. Just a minute ago, he was thinking, acting, hoping...Soon, however, he grasps the fact that the weapon which is pointing at him will not be diverted; and now, still breathing, he is simply matter; still thinking, he can think no longer. (ANTH 165)

And what about those who deploy force against others? People who imagine that they can wield force effectively without any deleterious effect on themselves are wrong: they become quickly intoxicated, blinded, and deformed by it as much as their victims. Being oriented to earthly power—and therefore, for Weil, against supernatural goodness—is the catalyst for becoming a *thing* on this side of force. She believed that we are free to choose our

Simone Weil

orientation and values in this world; Weil is no pre-determinist or even determinist. However, in choosing to pursue power for its own sake, we become ruled by mechanistic forces that are proper to objects. She explains through a typical analogy for her, gravitation:

> When, however, a man turns away from God [the good], he simply gives himself up to the law of gravity. Then he thinks that he can decide and choose, but he is only a thing, a stone that falls. If we examine human society and souls closely and with real attention, we see that wherever the virtue of supernatural light is absent, everything is obedient to mechanical laws as blind and as exact as the laws of gravitation. To know this is profitable and necessary. Those whom we call criminals are only tiles blown off a roof by the wind and falling at random. Their only fault is the initial choice by which they became such tiles.   (WG 75)

As for the play of power and use of force between nations or cultures, Weil saw no better illustration of its blind and brutal mechanisms than in the Greek historian and general Thucydides' description of the Athenians' destruction of Melos. The Athenians, who were at war with Sparta, sought to coerce the inhabitants of the little island of Melos (who had been allied to Sparta from antiquity but were remaining neutral) to join them. While the people of Melos invoked the ideals of justice in pleading their desire to remain neutral and wanting to protect their ancient civilization, it was unfortunately in vain:

> As they would not give in, the Athenians razed their city to the ground, put all their men to death, and sold all their women and children as slaves.
>
> Thucydides has put the lines in question into the mouth of these Athenians. They begin by saying that they will not try to prove that their ultimatum is just.
>
> 'Let us treat rather of what is possible. . . . You know it as well as we do; the human spirit is so constituted that what is just is only

examined if there is equal necessity on both sides. But if one is strong and the other weak, that which is possible is imposed by the first and accepted by the second.' (WG 86)

In other words, the natural law of power being described here shows that it functions like a necessary and mechanical reaction to perceived weakness; power expands and moves where *it can*, as if driven by a gravitational pull. To pursue 'what is possible' means that the strong will impose all it can upon the vulnerable; as Weil describes it, there is really just one will—that of the strong. Thus, between two or more people or groups who are unequal, power will be present and true justice will be impossible, at least on this 'natural' level. Of course, this is not an endorsement of this problematic dynamic—only a description.

While the ancient Greeks struggled with the perennial conundrum of the human condition, with its propensity for unchecked desire, it is worthwhile to recognize that social disequilibrium is perhaps more pervasive now than ever. Arguably, this is due in large part to the excesses and disparities inherent in late capitalist societies and our reinforced and socially approbated taste for unlimited accumulation of resources and amusements—forms of power that are frequently disguised and rationalized as 'guilty pleasures' or even 'self-care'. Weil comments on how we have lost an appreciation for temperance and measure in the contemporary world:

Modern life is *given over to excess*. Everything is steeped in it—thought as well as action, private life as well as public. (Sport: championships—pleasure to the point of intoxication and nausea—fatigue to the point of passing out—etc., etc., etc.).

(FLN 50)

In the ancient Greek writings she studied so extensively, Weil fixated on the stories, figures, and cultural practices that expressed a moderation we have since lost. For instance, in reading the tragedies of Aeschylus, Weil interpreted Zeus as 'the God of Moderation' and as one who was responsible for punishing excesses and abuses of power.

The ultimate lesson of many of these Greek tragedies was to understand our proper relationship to and place within the universe, as well as what constitutes a harmonious relationship with other people and within ourselves. Such understanding was premised upon a willingness to endure difficulty, and appropriately adjust to changing conditions, as well as a consent to natural limits. Weil expounds upon these lessons:

> The word [the Greeks] chose to designate suffering, πάθος [pathos], is one which evoked above all the idea of *enduring* much more than of suffering. Man must endure that which he does not want. He must find himself in submission to necessity. Misfortunes leave wounds which bleed drop by drop even during sleep; and thus, little by little, they break a man by violence and make him fit, in spite of himself, to receive wisdom, that wisdom which expresses itself as moderation. Man must learn to think of himself as a limited and dependent being, [and] suffering alone can teach him this. (IC 57)

In this light, our contemporary lack of equilibrium is undoubtedly tied to greater impatience, desire for immediate gratification, obsession with money and profiteering, and increased alienation from the world, others, and ourselves. Our disequilibrium is evident in many contexts: in imbalanced and anxious individual psyches, in the exploitative and non-reciprocal attitude of humans towards the natural world, between the demanding labour of the masses and their paltry compensations, and between the urgent needs of the vast majority of people and the obscene wealth and associated power of the oligarchs of the world. To bring about justice, the scales must be balanced, and Weil did not think this was possible without some inspiration that exceeds our 'natural' propensities towards acquiring and consuming the world.

Justice versus rights

For Weil, injustice is rooted in the human tendency towards egoism, greed, and self-protectionism that disregards the being of others—basically, dismissing the notion of limit or the ways in which others should serve as our limits. As she explains in her seminal essay, 'Human Personality' (*La Personne et le sacré*), every time someone sincerely cries out from the depths of their being, 'Why am I being hurt?', there is injustice present (ANTH 52). If this question arises from a misunderstanding, then the injustice consists in the inadequacy of the explanation provided to the one who is suffering. In other cases, the injustices stem from one of two primary motives. In the first case, a person may be deaf to cries of injury and pleas for explanation, and this deafness is often intentionally cultivated so that they can avoid any responsibility. That is, this form of injustice is banal and indicates moral laziness or deflective self-defensiveness. In the second case, injustice is found in the illegitimate and sometimes sadistic extension of one's limits, breaching the natural boundaries of others (e.g. in rape, slavery, exploitative work, colonialism, and so on). Thus, in any case, if injustice appears as a power-laden rupture of social equilibrium, then justice consists in being attentive and respecting limits: listening to and heeding the suffering of others, taking responsibility in our interdependent situations, and maintaining self-awareness and self-discipline to respect the boundaries and needs of others.

In unequal relationships, justice therefore entails relinquishing of power and prestige on the one side and a gracious reception on the other side. Enacting justice will frequently *feel* like disequilibrium, as people become accustomed to injustice as the status quo. Weil follows Plato in suggesting that humans are driven primarily by their appetites—base desires, like the desire to use other people for our own ends or to accumulate luxury. The establishment of justice in the inherently imbalanced natural world of human affairs requires something unnatural, or rather 'supernatural', as Weil thought.

Ultimately, attention infused with divine inspiration makes self-renunciation possible on the side of the powerful, which is necessary for what Weil calls the 'supernatural virtue of justice'. She explains: 'The supernatural virtue of justice consists of behaving exactly as though there were equality when one is stronger in an unequal relationship' (WG 87). And justice for the weaker side consists in gratitude for this refusal of the mechanisms of human power. To relinquish power where one could wield it over another is to do something that feels impossible; in a religious sense, it is to imitate the sacrifice of God, according to Weil. At times, she equivocates enacting justice with a kind of 'innocence', illustrated by the Passion of Christ:

> The Passion is purely supernatural justice, absolutely stripped of all sensible help, even of the love of God in so far as it can be felt.... To be innocent is to bear the weight of the entire universe. It is to throw away the counterweight. In emptying ourselves we expose ourselves to all the pressure of the surrounding universe. (GG 90, 91)

The problem with the Athenians as described by Thucydides, she thought, was that they assumed the gods (like humans) embraced power and took their ability to command others to the furthest extent possible. Weil also attributed this mistake to other religions, chiefly Judaism and Islam—perhaps erroneously. She found in Christianity a suffering, self-renouncing God which exemplified supernatural justice in her view. Those people who treat the vulnerable and powerless as equals recreate the 'original generosity of the Creator', the 'most Christian of virtues', according to her.

However, Weil also saw those virtues sublimely represented in the Egyptian Book of the Dead: 'I have never caused anyone to weep. I have never spoken with a haughty voice. I have never made

29

anyone afraid. I have never been deaf to words of justice and truth' (WG 88). Importantly, this sort of restraint upon our self-centred desires is simultaneously a gift of freedom for others. In fact, Weil writes that we have only recently invented the distinction between justice and love (*caritas*). As she explains,

> Only the absolute identification of justice and love makes the coexistence possible of compassion and gratitude on the one hand, and on the other, of respect for the dignity of affliction in the afflicted—a respect felt by the sufferer himself and the others. (WG 85)

The same thing cannot be said of 'rights', despite the fact that the two concepts are frequently treated as interchangeable. She noted that the Greeks had no conception of rights, nor did they even have the language to express it. They were entirely satisfied with the concept of justice (*dikē*), which inspired Weil in her critique of the discourse on rights.

What is the problem with rights? The framework of rights (as opposed to justice) evokes claims and counterclaims, a spirit of contention and contest, as well as inevitable exclusions: *I have a right to this, but not that; you have a right, but I don't have the right; if they have these rights, what about my rights to the same?* etc. Weil also believed that rights have no direct connection with love, whereas true justice, when enacted, reveals deep and loving attention to the suffering other(s). She also understood that rights are inherently proprietary, stemming from ancient Roman laws pertaining to the rightful use (or abuse) of property, a category which included certain human beings.

Weil illustrated the difference between rights and justice with a couple of important examples. One example is drawn from Sophocles' *Antigone*, where the title character epitomizes the upholding of transcendent and divine justice when she disobeys her tyrannical uncle Creon by honouring the death of her brother, who had turned against his country. Antigone explicitly cited the 'unwritten law' of Justice as her guide, against the earthly, discriminating edicts of her uncle. When Creon insisted, 'A foe is never a friend, not even in death', Antigone responded, 'I was born to share, not hate, but love' (ANTH 63). Weil saw the character of Antigone as an exemplar of profound, supernaturally inspired love, and she compared Antigone's higher calling and commitment to such 'extreme and absurd' love with that of Christ.

In another example, Weil describes how trying to coerce a farmer to sell their eggs at a moderate price might yield a response that invokes rights ('I have the right to set my prices'), but if a young girl is being forced into a brothel, the invocation of rights would sound 'ludicrously inadequate'. In general, she understood that dependence upon rights-claims relies upon the force of flawed human law and inhibits our finer impulses towards charity, love, and a sense of obligation to the spiritual, emotional, and physical needs of another—that is, the spirit of supernatural justice.

Contradiction and truth

To be just in this transcendent sense requires a deep attention not only to suffering others but also to the systems, institutions, and processes that structure our society and inform our values. In particular, attending to the connections between our own attitudes, decisions, and actions and the effects on others, alongside detaching from any self-centred desires, is crucial. One of the famous tests to discern a just person, the 'ring of Gyges' myth recounted in Plato's *Republic*, was interpreted by Weil in a rather unique way. In the myth, a shepherd discovered a gold ring within a cave and found that when he wore the ring and turned it on his finger, he became invisible. The question put to readers is whether a supposedly just person would remain virtuous with the power of invisibility, or whether they would fulfil their basest desires since there would be no penalties or sullied reputation.

In Weil's reading, the myth is about our ability to compartmentalize or 'set aside' our moral faults in relation to the consequences of those actions. Such setting aside is what enables people to do *anything* without a sense of shame, particularly when there are collective motivations and emotions at stake, like nationalism, patriotism, religious or partisan enthusiasms, or work/company zeal. In these sorts of contexts, the temptation to blind ourselves to our complicity in unjust doings is great. Weil provides an example of such a tendency, writing, 'The owner of a factory: "I enjoy such and such expensive pleasures, and my workmen suffer from poverty." He may be very sincerely sorry for his workmen, and yet not form the connection' (N 348). Moreover, she adds, we detest the people who show us the connections that we don't wish to make. Like the ancient Greeks, Weil understood that justice consists first of all in a willingness to *think*—to make connections between analogous things, even and especially when they indict us, or reveal our attachments to be problematic.

One method for cultivating a greater capacity for detachment is to meditate upon contraries and the ways in which there may be truth in their conjunction. Inspired by Pythagorean ideas, Weil contends that all truth contains a contradiction, and 'the good is always defined by the union of opposites' (N 447). While she admits that there are some unions of contraries that are bad or fallacious, particularly when the opposing terms occur on the same level with earthly values (e.g. the oppressed class being given the power to dominate over others), the proper union of opposites is achieved on a higher level and entails our suffering. The suffering is due to the detachment that is demanded of us, which often means attaching ourselves to a belief or thought that is incompatible with our initial belief. Hence in one of her paradoxical aphorisms, Weil notes, 'The union of contradictories means a spiritual quartering. It is by itself a passion, and is impossible without extreme suffering' (N 386). According to her, a classic instance of this higher union is found in the Gospel injunction, Matthew 5:44: 'But I tell you, love your enemies and pray for those who persecute you.'

There are several instances of contradiction (or at least paradox) in Weil's writings, including the following: the notion of a God who created the world by withdrawing; the idea that pure friendship is a harmony of necessity and liberty; the explicit belief in an absent God; the purification of the religious devotee by way of atheism; the effort of attention being a 'negative effort' that demands our mind's relaxation; the humbling of oneself being a moral elevation and, conversely, the raising of one's self being moral debasement; and so on. Contemplation of higher truths arises from positioning oneself at the uncomfortable intersection of our naturally limited and impure world with all of our fatigue and flaws and the sincere desire for pure, graceful, eternal values.

Weil understood this as a crucifixion of being and thought—the intersection of the horizontal necessities by the vertical possibilities for the good. Such is the position of mediators, like Socrates, Christ, and the saints. To negate the contradiction by being fully immersed in the world means that one has contented oneself with mediocre values, like rights and materialism. On the other hand, to be forgetful of the world in one's desires and prayers for the eternal values means that one has avoided their own responsibility in an interdependent landscape and taken the route of facile escapism. For Weil, in both scenarios there is illusion conferring pleasantness; but to desire Truth and Goodness from the proverbial cave is, as Plato described, an excruciating situation that will confuse us, temporarily blind us, demand a loosening of our strongest attachments, and require courage to face revelations that we cannot predict in a light to which we are hardly accustomed.

Desire for the good

Enlightened and properly oriented desire is presumed and necessary for any encounter with transcendent goodness or Truth according to Weil's philosophy. Her descriptions of desire (*eros*) and its role in an ethically attuned life are likewise inspired by

Greek thought, particularly Plato's 'middle dialogues' like *Symposium*, *Republic*, and *Phaedrus*, but, as with Plato, it is important to distinguish between 'enlightened desire' and what Weil sometimes calls 'base' or 'consumptive' desire. The former can lead one out of the metaphorical cave, while the latter keeps us shackled to an existence of shadows, illusions, deceptions, half-truths, and injustice. In her view, base desire is technically 'impossible', for 'it destroys its object' (N 421), meaning that such earthly desire is self-defeating because it consumes its object, thereby negating both the desired and the desiring.

Yet even this sort of lower desire is instructive about the human condition, and it also indicates something true about the nature of enlightened desire. It is a kind of energy directed towards something which the desirer lacks, revealing an incompleteness in the lover/desirer. As the classicist Anne Carson (who is greatly influenced by Weil) puts it, 'Who ever desires what is not gone? No one. The Greeks were clear on this. They invented eros to express it.' Desire, then, is an attraction founded on a sensible void, but this pull can be in relation to objects that are more or less noble or base. For both Weil and Plato, humans fundamentally desire the kind of wholeness characteristic of what is beautiful, true, and good (Weil reads this as synonymous with God); the problem is that we often confuse and conflate inferior/base objects with what is absolutely good—something Weil recognized as 'idolatry'. Evoking Plato's Allegory of the Cave, she writes, 'Idolatry comes from the fact that, while thirsting for absolute good, we do not possess the power of supernatural attention, and we have not the patience to allow it to develop.... Idolatry is thus a vital necessity in the cave' (GG 60).

It is constitutive of desire to seek to access and consume the objects of that desire; wanting is at least initially experienced as an urge to possess, even to *incorporate* into my being. Of course, as Weil realized, the paradox with desire is that as soon as we have the object of our desire, we no longer want it, by definition.

However, the pure and transcendent good, which we are sensibly drawn to, usually after being seduced by beauty, is a source of our erotic energy that, for one who is attentive, simultaneously compels a detached orientation towards the object which reflects this good. Weil, following Plato, contends that true beauty can transform our base desires and idolatrous tendencies (e.g. lust for physical bodies, for monetary rewards, for political power, etc.) into noble desires for the good, and this transformation will also cultivate a contemplative attitude in the desiring subject.

For Weil, it is imperative, then, that we fasten onto this sort of attraction, for it implies moral attention and brings about behaviour that respects the integrity and freedom of others. The question is whether we are able to recognize glimpses of absolute beauty or goodness in the world; if we do not or cannot see beauty piercing through what we love (or for Plato, if our souls have *forgotten* the forms of Beauty and Goodness), then there is nothing to hold us back in our quest to consume; we see only opportunities for our own gratification. Furthermore, Weil says that we must

> go down to the source of our desires in order to tear the energy away from its object. It is there that desires are true, in so far as they are energy. It is the object which is false. But there is an indescribable wrenching apart of the soul at the separation of a desire from its object. (N 203–4)

We know that this detachment, this wrenching apart, is the condition of truth, for Weil. And when she says that the object is 'false' she means that, because of the overreaching nature of our desire (which is really aimed at a transcendent good), we often *project* qualities of the absolute upon what is limited and relative; we deceive ourselves about the people and things that we love in an effort to convince ourselves that we will have some sort of final and permanent satisfaction. Thus, it is necessary that we check our attachments to the things and beings of this world with the lucidity of mindful contextualization and proportionate thinking, insofar as our desires tend to be infused with outsized illusions.

In the well-known story that the comic Aristophanes told in Plato's *Symposium*, when the two human 'halves' find their respective missing half after roaming the ends of the earth, they immediately cling to one another, seem to belong to one another, and never want to be apart. 'These are the people who finish out their lives together and still cannot say what it is they want from one another,' Plato writes through the voice of Aristophanes. That is, despite having found what we believed we were ultimately searching for (e.g. that other person who perfectly 'completes' us), Aristophanes notes that 'it's obvious that the soul of every lover longs for something else; his soul cannot say what it is, but like an oracle it has a sense of what it wants, and like an oracle it hides behind a riddle.' Weil also describes our general insatiability as humans, writing, 'One always wants something more', but also: 'We have only to imagine all our desires satisfied; after a time we should become discontented. We should want something else and we should be miserable through not knowing what to want' (SNL 148).

This 'something else' is, for both Plato and Weil, 'the good forever', or immortality. But again, we too often make the mistake of ascribing limitlessness to limited beings. Do we not cast our loved ones in the rosiest of lights, downplaying their faults and mediocrities? How often do we imbue the *idea* of a person we love with all of the values we hold dear, disregarding the reality of that person? There is a strong and perpetual temptation to see only what we wish to see and to deny the rest. Thus, Weil explains that tearing our desire away from finite beings involves a difficult thought experiment: 'Never to think of a thing which we cannot actually see without thinking that perhaps it has been destroyed. Let such a thought not dissipate the sense of reality, but render it more intense' (N 218–19). More than being some morbid meditation, this strategy is representative of the kind of sober reality-checking we must continually practise to liberate eros (and our consumptive, controlling tendencies) from those objects/ persons we tend to fictionalize by wrapping them in our fantasies and reorient it towards what is *actually* infinite—which cannot be an experienced object for us. Otherwise, we are engaging in idolatry.

It is clear, then, that Weil advocates fixating onto enlightened desire *as such*, for when we really attend to the objects of our love *as they are*, in our unsentimental state we find that their reality is sufficient to detach us from the obsession with having or overpowering. While the objects may be illusory, in our way of wanting them, the desire or hunger we feel is ultimately for the good and therefore is very real. Taken to its fullest logical extent, this is a recommendation to embrace a kind of object-less, empty desire for goodness and justice, and then to wait for truth to reveal itself to us. Let us not forget that Plato was, after all, a mystic for Weil. As she saw it, 'The wisdom of Plato is not a philosophy, a search for God by means of human reason. Such research was made as well as it can be made by Aristotle. Plato's wisdom is nothing but an orientation of the soul towards grace' (IC 85).

Chapter 3
Labour and politics

Simone Weil's deep sensitivity to instances of injustice and abuse of power is manifest across all of her writings, but her political concerns—which always include the plight of the working classes and conditions of labour—are particularly emphasized in works like *Oppression and Liberty*, her autobiographical 'Factory Journal', *On the Abolition of All Political Parties*, and *The Need for Roots*. *Oppression and Liberty* consists of a set of essays, written between 1932 and 1934, that were posthumously collected by Albert Camus, who admired her so greatly that he named her as a major inspiration in his Nobel Prize address. One of these, 'Reflections concerning the Causes of Liberty and Social Oppression', is a combination of a masterful analysis of conditions for dignified labour, a sympathetic critique of Marx and Marxism, an examination of oppression in its relation to certain types of work, and an outline for the foundation of a free society. It is in this essay that we find Weil's unflinching assessment of her contemporary social-political milieu, which she characterized as completely imbalanced:

> Never has the individual been so completely delivered up to a blind collectivity, and never have men been less capable, not only of subordinating their actions to their thoughts, but even of thinking. Such terms as oppressors and oppressed, the idea of classes—all that sort of thing is near to losing all meaning, so obvious are the

impotence and distress of all men in face of the social machine, which has become a machine for breaking hearts and crushing spirits, a machine for manufacturing irresponsibility, stupidity, corruption, slackness and, above all, dizziness. The reason for this painful state of affairs is perfectly clear. We are living in a world in which nothing is made to man's measure; there exists a monstrous discrepancy between man's body, man's mind and the things which at the present time constitute the elements of human existence; everything is disequilibrium.   (OL 108)

Weil understood the importance of governing bodies, social practices, customs, and opportunities for work and relationality that are scaled to reflect human needs in an ideal society, but what she observed in early 20th-century France was a society geared more towards machines, profit, and efficiency than persons. That such environments and infrastructure have become increasingly specialized, technical, and bureaucratic has been a primary factor in a number of disruptive social trends characterizing the 20th and, now, the 21st century, including more dehumanizing and alienating work, greater political impotence and cynicism among ordinary citizens, increased ignorance about systemic economic influences and individual fiscal limits, and the subordination of human creativity to automation.

Work and oppression

By 1934 Weil was convinced that there was little chance of meaningful societal change through political activism, especially in light of something she called 'a new species of oppression', the faceless and centralized bureaucracies that had come to inhabit the modern state and its industries. At the same time, she still fervently believed that the relative liberation of the workers was essential in addressing this widespread oppression and creating a truly *free* working class. She understood that grasping the real conditions for worker liberation required actually experiencing the current situation of workers. For this reason, Weil took a year of unpaid leave from her comfortable philosophy teaching position in Le Puy, France, to seek this other kind of labour, and she found work in the factories of Alsthom, Carnaud, and Renault to help her make 'contact with real life' (Figure 5). Only in this way, she thought, could she move beyond superficial diagnoses of the workers' predicaments to fully understand the relationship between humans and the world, between culture and modern technology, and to clarify the values of productivity and progress in regards to human capacities and needs. In December 1934, she was interviewed for her first position by Auguste Detœuf, the director of the Alsthom Electrical Engineering Works factory, the largest manufacturer of electric equipment in France.

5. End of shift at the Renault auto plant, where Weil worked in 1935.

In a letter to a student of hers, right after she began work at the Alsthom factory in spring 1935, she described the value she was discovering in this work: 'Above all, I feel I have escaped from a world of abstractions, to find myself among real people—some good and some bad, but with a real goodness or badness' (SL 11). She went on to say that any trace of kindness or intelligence in the factory is remarkable and probably genuine, since there is widespread fatigue and 'one is paid not to think' (SL 12). Weil also admitted that she was fortunate in not being compelled by necessity to work in the factories, especially since the situation for women in factories was dire: they were almost always relegated to purely mechanical and dehumanizing labour, in which the main thing required of them was speed and dexterity.

In the early 20th century, Frederick Winslow Taylor's organizational schemes were being fully deployed in factories to monitor, regulate, predict, and prescribe the minutest of workers' movements within certain time-frames. Weil was well aware of the dominance of Taylorism in the factories and the degree to which this system was responsible for dehumanizing people as a result of the connection of wages to productivity via 'time and motion' studies, linked to the speed and output of the individual worker. French trade union leader Alphonse Merrheim had said that Taylorism 'eliminated, annihilated and banished personality, intelligence, even the very desires of the workers, from the workshops and factories'. Yet Taylorism was intended and believed by some to be a humanist shift in work organization, insofar as it sought to increase the yield of work without increasing the exhaustion of the worker, and therefore to increase the worker's wages by a considerable amount.

Weil learned very quickly after she began her work at Alsthom, which consisted of drilling washers repeatedly, that such humanist dreams were not being realized. For instance, it was nearly impossible to sustain any sort of substantive thinking process or meaningful attention while trying to keep up with the demanded speed on the assembly line: 'The effect of exhaustion is to make me forget my real reasons for spending time in the factory, and to make it almost impossible for me to overcome the strongest temptation that this life entails: that of not thinking anymore, which is the one and only way of not suffering from it' (FW 171). That is, any reflective activity is practically precluded by the incessant, repetitive motions and sensory harnessing necessitated by the productivity imperatives in the factory environment. Thought requires leisure. Weil remarked that it was only on Sundays, when she experienced some prolonged time free from work, that 'memories and shreds of ideas return[ed]' to her. She realized that romantic notions of revolt during the workweek are basically impossible, except as momentary feelings, for the isolation and individualism on the assembly line may pit the worker against her tools, but usually pits the workers against each other.

Docility, not enlightened revolutionary energy, is the effect of the factory environment. As Weil wrote in her *Factory Journal* in her seventh week at Alsthom, 'We are like horses who hurt themselves as soon as they pull on their bits—and we bow our heads. We even lose consciousness of the situation; we just submit. Any reawakening of thought is then painful' (FW 171). Moreover, there is a lack of a sense of purpose in the work, and even a lack of knowledge of the ultimate product or vision to which one is contributing. Orders from superiors frequently seem arbitrary or impossible to fulfil. Incentives to endure the mechanical and monotonous work are of the lowest sort—usually easily quantifiable things like money, lunch, or small windows of free time, rather than ambitions for widespread social change (which would be very difficult for the unskilled worker to imagine, given their conditioned and reinforced docility). Such base rewards provide a minimum of energy necessary to renew the motivation that was depleted by work. But often the paycheck or the time off was so meagre that it barely sustained the ability to return to work. Still, she discovered that workers attach all importance to these paltry compensations, for they feel impotent to change the other conditions and are often too timid to ask for anything else.

Weil recognized that even 'free time' was no guarantee of liberation for a worker. She noted that a 'foreman can impose a method of working, or defective tools, or a rhythm of work, such as to produce an excess of fatigue which makes all one's hours *outside* the factory a blank' (SL 56). This means that non-work time cannot be truly enjoyed, as it is essentially annexed by the brutal working conditions that require more of the human body and mind than what is possible to give within the workday. Breaks and holidays are therefore structured in service to the work, leading to the most profound forms of alienation. Weil, who was known to admire Charlie Chaplin, once remarked to Detœuf that the feeding-machine depicted in *Modern Times* is 'the most perfect and truest symbol of the workers' position in the factory' (SL 58) (Figure 6).

In short, to work in the factory is to experience an extreme form of humiliation, even to the point of affliction (*malheur*). For Weil, affliction is a phenomenon beyond simple suffering. It includes the sense of utter degradation, general social exclusion, the inability to communicate one's inhuman situation to others, and usually the distinctive feeling of God's abandonment (if one is religious)—or at least complete hopelessness. To be unable to verbalize such a horrible state adds to the deep isolation entailed by affliction: 'Affliction is by its nature inarticulate. The afflicted silently beseech to be given the words to express themselves' (ANTH 65). Factory workers, for instance, intimately know that registering complaints about their conditions will not improve their situation; rather, it will probably only make their lives worse. So, they internalize their despair and anger until they become insensitive to the fact of their oppression and may even convince themselves of the nobility of their work and generosity of their supervisors. Weil captures this phenomenon poignantly:

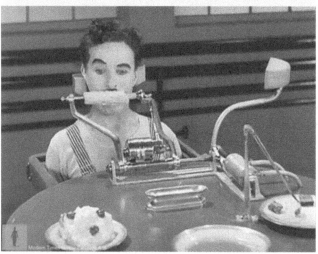

6. Charlie Chaplin and the 'Billows Feeding Machine' from *Modern Times* (1936), comically representing the kind of dehumanizing automation of which Weil was critical.

By carrying oppression beyond a certain point, the powerful inevitably make their slaves *adore* them. Because the thought of being in absolute subjection as somebody's plaything is a thought no human being can sustain: so if a man is left with no means at all of escaping constraint he has no alternative except to persuade himself that he is doing voluntarily the very things he is forced to do; in other words, he substitutes *devotion* for *obedience*... (FLN 41)

This observation applies to any situation of oppression—not just alienating factory work. In general, beyond the hardships imposed and devaluation of human lives, a major tragedy of oppression, for Weil, is the antipathy towards thinking. It is not only the oppressed who are tempted to 'lapse into unconsciousness' so as not to suffer greatly, but also the oppressors are tempted by delusions of their own greatness. For both sides, there is an incentive to suppress thought. 'One can be in a prison cell and in chains,' Weil writes, 'but one can also be smitten with blindness and paralysis. There is no difference' (GG 157).

Critique of Marxism

Through her time working in the factories, Weil realized that workers' revolts would not bring an end to the humiliation and affliction they experienced in those environments. In the first place, she was dubious that any sort of meaningful revolt would be initiated: 'Revolt is impossible, except in momentary flashes (I mean even as a feeling). First of all, against what? You are alone with your work, you could not revolt except against it—but to work in an irritated state of mind would be to work badly, and therefore to starve' (FW 171). Not only did Weil find it difficult to imagine revolt for the degraded, desperate, and exhausted worker, but she also was critical of the Marxian notion of 'revolution' itself, understood as the reversal of forces such that the weak could be victorious over the powerful. Such a reversal does not actually change the problematic nature of *force*, which for her was an intoxicating means to power that sidestepped thought and attention. In fact, she believed that the attempt at revolt—particularly if it is unsuccessful—could contribute to the power of the oppressor through the ensuing feelings of impotence and despair in the oppressed classes.

The central problem with Marxism, Weil thought, is that it ushers in a dangerous fantasy for workers while ignoring their lived experiences of exhaustion and humiliation. In 'Reflections Concerning the Causes of Liberty and Social Oppression', she writes that we must have sufficient 'intellectual courage to ask ourselves if the term "revolution" is anything else but a name, if it has any precise content' (OL 39). The idea of revolution, that is, functions largely as just that—*an idea*, which is compensatory for the sufferings produced by inhuman conditions. 'It is ambition translated into the collective, the crazy ambition of the ascent of all workers out of the workers' condition', she wrote (LPW 133). She worried that the intoxicating nature of power and the 'need for adventure' would transform a revolt against injustice into 'a worker imperialism entirely analogous to national imperialism', thus undermining the workers' integrity and their righteous arguments against the injustices of capitalism. Just as Marx warned against religion as an 'opiate of the masses', Weil found that 'the hope of revolution is always a drug' (LPW 134).

At the same time, Weil did not think Marx's political theory should be wholly disregarded. To the contrary, she found two major contributions from Marx which she called 'solid, indestructible': one is his method of making society an object of study through analysing the relationships of force therein, and the other is his critical assessment of capitalist society as it existed in the 19th century. She agreed with his formidable discovery that the essence of capitalism was rooted in the subordination of subjects to objects, of persons to things, bringing about forms of alienation hitherto unknown. While she appreciated this definition of capitalism along with his method of examining social relationships through the lens of force, she did find that some of his conclusions were overdetermined because of the historical context in which he was writing, which tended to uncritically esteem progressive narratives of history.

For Weil, it was a mistake to neglect an eternal, spiritual order which would enable the human spirit to transcend the shifting social mechanics structured around force. This did not mean that she thought organized religion or a notion of God should be a pacifier for the afflicted; in fact, she believed that materialism had been deified and 'Marxism [had] always possessed a religious character' (OL 163). She grasped the danger inherent in posing a seductive salve—whether collective uprising or a promise of heaven—to the desperate masses. The problem with Marxism in particular, she claimed, is that 'it is a religion devoid of *mystique*'.

What is 'mystique'? It seems that what Weil was seeking to express was the importance of the intangible and unobjectifiable *good* that the working classes (and indeed, all people) crave in their quest for justice. To keep the analysis of the social problem, along with its resolution, on the material level, as Marx did, is necessarily to replicate the same dynamics and struggle for liberty, over and over. 'The human soul's longing for liberty, its craving for power, can equally well be analysed as facts of a spiritual order', she wrote (OL 162). Even though he rightly understood the workers' thirst for absolute justice and the ways in which they were oppressed by the blind mechanisms of technological 'progress' and bourgeois fantasies, Marx was 'an idolater', Weil wrote. The object of his idolatry was not only an imagined 'society of the future', but also the proletariat itself. In her view, he had accepted a logical absurdity:

> [Marx] assumed that, though everything is governed by force, a proletariat lacking force was nevertheless going to carry through a successful political *coup d'état*, follow it up by a purely legal measure, namely the abolition of individual property, and as a result achieve the mastery in all fields of social life. (OL 161–2)

His mistake in thinking, Weil surmised, could be attributable to the sense of prestige that accompanies an appearance of force; even Marx could not resist that appeal. It was a puerile thought, she argued, that force can simply change hands such that one day, the weak (being morally unchanged) will have force on their side and oppression will cease to exist. The truth is, Weil argued, when force changes hands, there is still a relation of dominance intact. Marx could not escape this essential contradiction:

> In short, Marx's revolutionary materialism consists in positing, on the one hand, that force alone governs social relations to the exclusion of anything else, and, on the other hand, that one day the weak, while remaining the weak, will nevertheless be the stronger. He believed in miracles without believing in the supernatural.

> (OL 158–9)

Political rhetoric and parties

Weil's critique of Marx's idolization of the proletariat also stemmed from her suspicion of *collectivities* and their overly simplistic rhetoric, symbols, and claims. A collectivity (or collective) is Weil's term for a large group of people united under an identity, usually political, cultural, or religious in nature; for instance, a political party or a religious denomination would constitute a collective. She grasped that collectivities have a strong allure for individuals given the kind of pride, prestige, sense of belonging, and moral righteousness that a collective confers on a person. Weil even admitted to the temptation posed by some of the most notorious collectivities, like the Nazi Party. In a letter to Father Joseph-Marie Perrin in 1942, Weil described her fear of the Catholic Church as a 'social structure', given her disposition to be too easily influenced by collectives. To emphasize her point, she continued: 'I know that if at this moment I had before me a group of twenty young Germans singing Nazi songs in chorus, a part of my soul would instantly become Nazi' (WG 11). While clearly opposed to Nazi ideology and practices, Weil was expressing the strong pull that collectives, like churches and political groups, exercise over individuals.

In her view, the major problem with a collectivity is that it represents an ersatz good or divinity. That is, collectivities are false imitations of transcendent goodness (or God), and therefore they constitute the 'object of all idolatry', attracting patriotism, feelings of absolute loyalty, and uncritical, blindly obedient dispositions. Collectivities are therefore dangerous, given their influence and power over thinking subjects. For this reason, Weil compared the collective to Plato's myth of the 'Great Beast' as described in his *Republic*. To fall under the spell of the Great Beast is to think and act in conformity with the prejudices of the multitude, compromising one's own intellectual honesty and search for truth. Not surprisingly, Weil eschewed collectivities of any kind, refusing church as well as party membership, even if she had sympathies with some of the views of various collectives:

> I do not want to be adopted into a circle, to live among people who say 'we' and to be part of an 'us', to find I am 'at home' in any human *milieu* whatever it may be. In saying I do not want this, I am expressing myself badly, for I should like it very much; I should find it all delightful. But I feel that it is not permissible for me. I feel that it is necessary and ordained that I should be alone, a stranger and an exile in relation to every human circle without exception. (WG 13)

At first glance, such a declaration of self-imposed isolation seems to be at odds with Weil's desire to lose herself among the masses so as to know and love people as they are, without pretences. However, this desire, for Weil, implies a detachment that would prevent her from having a sense of belonging or developing an identity in relation to any organization. Therefore, while Weil's words and actions expressed solidarity with the working classes and often reflected a Christian inspiration, she unequivocally proclaimed her independence from any religious or party membership. With respect to the latter, in 1943, the last year of her life, she wrote an essay translated as *On the Abolition of All Political Parties*. In this incisive essay, she identified three essential characteristics of a political party:

> 1. A political party is a machine to generate collective passions.
>
> 2. A political party is an organization designed to exert collective pressure upon the minds of all its individual members.
>
> 3. The first objective and also the ultimate goal of any political party is its own growth, without limit. (APP 11)

Crucially, what follows from these three primary characteristics, Weil argued, is that 'every party is totalitarian—potentially, and by aspiration'. Those who have paid attention and/or who have been involved with a political party could testify to the veracity of these points, Weil thought.

Insofar as a political party rouses the enthusiasms of the multitude to increase its membership, control, and power, it must also be necessarily vague with regard to its doctrine. Vague doctrines enable a party to expand its reach and serve as a kind of Rorschach inkblot test for prospective members in which they can project their own psychologies and dogmas without resistance. As Weil explains, 'The goal of a political party is something vague and unreal. If it were real, it would demand a great effort of attention, for the mind does not easily encompass the concept of the public interest' (APP 13). The party then becomes its own end, rather than the public good, and no amount of power attained will ever be deemed sufficient, for there is always more power to be had.

While a political party will give lip service to the public interest, such statements always amount to a fiction, 'an empty shell devoid of all reality', according to Weil. If the doctrines and speeches actually concerned reality, they would be subject to limits and qualifications—an unappealing fact for a group bent on growth at all costs. But since what is devoid of existence cannot by definition encounter any limitations, there is a natural affinity between the power-hungry collectives and fabrications or empty speech. This is the case for practically all political rhetoric.

Political collectivities therefore necessarily use empty signifiers, or what Weil called 'words with capital letters', in their messages and propaganda. Such vague but emotionally charged words and phrases generate the collective passions that eclipse individual thought. Such phrases—like 'national interest', 'freedom', 'communism', 'democracy', 'capitalism', 'family values', 'woke', 'law and order', etc.—are employed by politicians without much substance or precise definition. Because of this fact, the words are 'all swollen with blood and tears', heavy with emotion and association, but they are also vacuous. Meanwhile, 'words with content and meaning are not murderous', Weil writes. However:

> ...when empty words are given capital letters, then, on the slightest pretext, men will begin shedding blood for them and piling up ruin in their name, without effectively grasping anything to which they refer, since what they refer to can never have any reality, for the simple reason that they mean nothing. In these conditions, the only definition of success is to crush a rival group of men who have a hostile word on their banners; for it is characteristic of these empty words that each of them has its complementary antagonist.
>
> (ANTH 221)

It is clear that 'words with capital letters' are dangerous tools of political parties. The antidote to such instigation of collective passions is clear, painstaking definition of terms—and thinking, in general. Properly defined words cannot easily serve as slogans in a bid for power. As Weil rightly noted, 'To clarify thought, to discredit the intrinsically meaningless words, and to define the use of others by precise analysis—to do this, strange though it may appear, might be a way of saving human lives' (ANTH 222).

If political parties and their empty rhetoric are responsible for the devaluation and devastation of the common good and true justice across a society, then what constitutes the ideal society? To answer this difficult question, Weil takes up the task of outlining the needs of the human soul. Only after this essential understanding of the psyche is gained can she begin to elaborate the aspirational polis to which we can be meaningfully rooted.

Needs of the soul and the ideal society

For Weil, rescuing society from the forces contributing to disequilibrium and dehumanization resides in attending to the basic needs of the human psyche and attempting to raise and implement those values into decentralized and collaborative governing processes. Admittedly, she was not optimistic about the likelihood of this realization.

> The only possibility of salvation would lie in a methodical co-operation between all, strong and weak, with a view to accomplishing a progressive decentralization of social life; but the absurdity of such an idea strikes one immediately. Such a form of co-operation is impossible to imagine, even in dreams, in a civilization that is based on competition, on struggle, on war.... What weight can the hopes and desires of those who are not at the control levers carry, when, reduced to the most tragic impotence, they find themselves the mere playthings of blind and brutish forces? (OL 120)

Ultimately, then, Weil's prescriptions for centring human dignity in social practices and policies were more modest than large-scale economic transformations. To the question *What can we do to dignify the human spirit in an alienating society?* Weil responds, 'Nothing, except endeavor to introduce a little play into the cogs of the machine that is grinding us down', as well as awaken thought where we are able and support other individuals' ability to think and act with integrity (OL 121).

Improving the material conditions of workers may be important but insufficient to address the oppressive situations that preclude individuals' abilities to think and be attentive to the world. A factory worker who makes a higher wage than she did previously will still feel alienated and uprooted as a result of the type of work in which she is engaged. This is because certain of her essential human needs are still being neglected. In *The Need for Roots*, Weil tells us that we all have 'eternal obligations' towards our fellows that correspond with vital human needs, including physical needs as well as needs of the soul. Some of our physical needs are: food and water, protection against violence, housing, clothing, heating, hygiene, and medical attention in cases of illness. We also have indirect obligations to things like a wheatfield because it generates food for humans.

We also have other needs that are integral to the vitality of the soul which Weil says we must take care not to confuse with 'desires, whims, fancies, and vices'. According to her, the needs of the soul include order, liberty, obedience, responsibility, equality, hierarchism, honour, punishment, freedom of opinion, security, risk, private property, collective property, and truth. Needless to say, each of these needs requires elaboration (which Weil provides in *The Need for Roots*), particularly as there are apparent contraries in the list, like liberty and obedience. Let us contemplate this pair in connection with Weil's sketch of an ideal society.

Liberty, according to Weil, is the ability to choose so that there is complete integrity of conscience. But liberty does not exist in a vacuum. In the context of a community, we know that rules are imposed for the common good which must necessarily limit the possibilities of choice for each person. Therefore, obedience to established rules is also a primary need of the human psyche, as is a sense of responsibility for others. Nor does obedience exempt leaders from the need to be accountable. Obedience presupposes consent to the general good of society, not so that every single command will be carried out thoughtlessly, but in general, for accountability to the community. Obedience in this sense implies a consent to limits and the willingness to answer to the higher good, beyond the self.

True liberty does not entail, therefore, the absence of all constraint or necessity; hers is not a negative freedom but a positive freedom akin to relational consent. It is 'not defined by a relationship between desire and its satisfaction, but by a relationship between thought and action; the absolutely free man would be he whose every action proceeded from a preliminary judgment concerning the end which he set himself and the sequence of means suitable for attaining this end' (OL 85). Weil admits that this kind of liberty is an ideal which can steer us, even if it cannot be perfectly achieved.

In applying this idea of liberty to the complexities of contemporary society, it becomes clear that part of this 'steering' towards an ideal will be found in more liberated forms of work, through the recognition that human labour is always subject to necessity, a wellspring for thought grounded in reality. That is, human dignity can be respected in giving our free consent to the necessities and rhythms of the natural world, in contrast to the forceful and arbitrary mandates and unnatural speeds characterizing the oppressive factory work that effectively alienated people and paralysed thought. Weil remarked that it seemed machines were being expected to 'do the thinking', while the humans who served them were 'reduced to the condition of automata' (OL 92). Instead of this, Weil proposed two types of liberated work for post-war France in which people could be 'rooted' in the natural world of necessity: small artisanal workshops that could prevail over production; and something Weil called 'spiritual labour', in which labourers would work in harmony with the rhythms of the natural earth. This vision provides a glimpse into Weil's broader project of describing an ideal 'rooted' society in which citizens respect natural limits and orient themselves towards transcendent goodness.

In the first example of liberated work, the workshop artisans would be experts in their crafts, enjoying the respect that comes from expression of their talents. They would have a meaningful focus while also understanding the whole product/vision to which their work contributes. Their workshops would be communal and would allow different artisans to collaborate, share ideas, and work in tandem to bring about the best product for the needs of society, while respecting the artisans' expert knowledge, time, and physical limitations. In the second case, the rhythms of 'spiritual labour' are to be found in activities like farm work, in which one's own body must be in touch with impersonal organic processes and growth cycles. This sort of work is itself a mediation between the natural forces of life and the supernatural values of humility, obedience, and equilibrium. Labour, that is, should be the 'spiritual core' of a well-ordered social life, as it keeps us in touch with the limitations of time, our own physical capabilities, and other material realities.

In general, the society Weil envisioned at the end of her short life was one that in many ways reclaimed the value of a collectivity but under certain conditions. She argued for our 'need for roots'—a kind of connection between the realities and necessities of earthly life with its natural limitations and the ideal of supernatural justice that serves as a guide. She recognized that humans need to feel vital, purposeful, and active in relation to the life of their community and their cultural/social traditions, while working towards implementing eternal values. In this way, a collectivity may be redeemed as a mode of establishing roots within a community as long as it fosters attentive relationships and a 'new patriotism' based on compassion and a desire for truth.

As Weil writes, 'The world requires at the present time a new patriotism. And it is now that this inventive effort must be made, just when patriotism is something which is causing bloodshed' (NR 145). Such a patriotism will not consist in absolute loyalty to earthly rulers, parties, or nations. But this new patriotism will be grounded in a dedication to a higher good, a reality outside this world that inspires all beauty, truth, justice, legitimacy, and the recognition in us that we are obliged to remedy, according to our abilities, 'all the privations of soul and body which are liable to destroy or damage the earthly life of any human being whatsoever' (ANTH 205).

Chapter 4
Religion

Simone Weil's approach to religion and religious belief has been the source of much commentary and debate in the years since her death. Questions have tended to focus on issues such as: what Christian faith meant to Weil; the status of her mystical experiences; her apparent antipathy for Judaism; and the extent to which she embraced atheism. She was undoubtedly a religious and arguably a Christian thinker, even if she was wary of institutionalized religion. However, *religiosity* is capable of transcending institution (and, in fact, its purest forms may be the antithesis of the institutional manifestations), so resistance to the organizations and collectivisms of religion did not prevent Weil from affirming the beauty, truth, and goodness that arise from various religions, especially Christianity. As this chapter will endeavour to demonstrate, Weil's religious philosophy is not based on explicit doctrines or dogmas but is rather 'a conception of human life', reflecting both her lived experiences and her belief that the finite, suffering, force-centred world cannot be all there is.

Desiring the transcendent and absolute good is the foundation for Weil's notion of religiosity. She thought that religion is, at its core, a 'promise of God' that anyone who sincerely contemplates and desires the supernatural can be wholly transformed. Therefore, we will consider Weil's unique Christian understanding and mystical experiences; her approach to the problem of evil and related concepts like decreation; the inspirations provided by other religious traditions, like Taoism, Hinduism, and Buddhism, as well as her notorious antipathy towards Judaism; and, finally, her endorsement of a certain form of atheism as a means of religious purification.

Implicit Christianity and mystical experiences

Weil was raised in an agnostic and secular Jewish home, but she would later suggest that she felt she had received the 'Christian inspiration' early in her life and had been 'born inside' the Christian community without any human intervention. Such a long-standing affinity to a Christian worldview (alongside her attraction to other religious traditions, like Hinduism and Buddhism) was traceable to several of her interests, including: her penchant for purity in thought and action, the appeal of the idea of self-sacrifice, her philosophical vocation to seek truth, her positive valuation of humility, her desire to understand affliction, and her endeavour to love the entire world—all of which required an impersonal, selfless outlook. Weil's religiosity in general and her Christian orientation in particular was always a matter of her desire to be in contact with *the real* rather than as a response to any fear of mortality or need for an overarching narrative to give meaning to the inexplicable in human existence. In fact, religion used to placate existential dis-ease constituted an illegitimate and dangerous practice, Weil thought, for in this sense it is little more than a self-catering and consoling fiction.

Writing in her 'Spiritual Autobiography' to Father Joseph-Marie Perrin in 1942, Weil noted that she never 'sought for God', but instead understood 'the problem of God as a problem the data of which could not be obtained here below' (WG 22). Philosophical-theological arguments will not resolve the question of God's existence and in this sense are pragmatically futile. As a result, she thought the best approach to such questions was to leave them alone, neither affirming nor denying anything, but remaining open to what might reveal itself to an attentive disposition. Despite not explicitly engaging the question of God or religious dogma, Weil recognized that her outlook and conception of life was probably always a Christian one. But in what sense?

To begin with, she distinctly felt the vocational urge to pursue truth from an early age. Comparing herself to her brother André, the mathematical genius, caused a great sense of inferiority and an abiding depression when she was young. Yet in the midst of this dark period, Weil had the epiphany that any human being could 'penetrate to the kingdom of truth reserved for genius, if only he longs for truth and perpetually concentrates all his attention upon its attainment' (WG 23). She named this attentive longing for truth *prayer*, believing that the sincere and unadulterated desire for truth would lead one to make contact with God. She wrote to Father Perrin, 'Christ likes us to prefer truth to him because, before being Christ, he is truth. If one turns aside from him to go toward the truth, one will not go far before falling into his arms' (WG 27). In other words, she grasped a distinctive relationship between desire for truth/beauty/goodness (or the philosophic quest) and the reception of grace, which may come in the form of Christ. But the emphasis is decisively placed upon an agnostic and intense search for truth, distinct from an a priori adherence to a concept of God under which other findings are subordinated, distorted, or religiously rationalized.

At the same time, Weil realized that her vocation, which was a calling to be intellectually honest to the highest degree, necessitated that she remain outside the Catholic Church and detached from its dogmas. The Church's powerful spirit of collectivism, its historical abuses committed against the vulnerable in the name of salvation, its exclusion of diverse peoples and cultures, and the blind acceptance of doctrine would compromise the integrity of her quest for truth. Thus, Weil refused to become a part of the official organization or to partake in its sacred rites, like baptism or the Eucharist.

Weil also interpreted her early passion for justice and love of neighbour as a 'Christian idea'. These concerns intersected with her admiration for the spirit of poverty and her desire to know first hand the experiences of the working underclasses in France. In 1935, following her year in the factories, Weil took a trip with her parents to Portugal where, one evening in a small village by herself, she observed the wives of fishermen singing 'ancient hymns of heart-rending sadness' and carrying candles in a procession while making a tour of the ships. Feeling mentally exhausted and still physically wrecked from her time in the factories, Weil felt this contact with affliction [*malheur*] had effectively ended her youth. Such contact with hellish reality instilled in her the sense of absolute degradation and slavery to necessity. As a result, she was struck with the idea that 'Christianity is pre-eminently the religion of slaves, that slaves cannot help belonging to it, and I among others' (WG 26). The feeling that one is mere matter, indistinguishable from the anonymous multitudes who are also suffering, was a uniquely Christian experience for Weil. As readers will likely recognize, this is a vision of Christianity that is diametrically opposed to the feel-good, self-affirming, capitalistic versions of some contemporary Christian denominations and worldviews, such as those influenced by the 'prosperity gospel'.

Her other two significant religious experiences would occur in Assisi and Solesmes. In Assisi in 1937, in a little 12th-century Romanesque chapel, she would feel compelled to pray for the first time. In Solesmes, France, a year later, Weil and her mother attended Holy Week services at a monastery (Figure 7). Weil was suffering from excruciating migraines, but she was able to find 'a pure and perfect joy in the unimaginable beauty of the chanting and the words', which allowed her to grasp the possibility of experiencing divine love in the midst of affliction.

While in Solesmes, she met a young English Catholic man who introduced her to the English metaphysical poets, including

7. Solesmes Benedictine Abbey of Saint-Pierre, where Simone Weil attended the holy services during Easter week of 1938.

George Herbert. Weil memorized Herbert's poem 'Love' and would frequently recite it, like a prayer, in the midst of her headaches. During one of these recitations, she reports that 'Christ came down and took possession of me' (WG 27). For her this contact was unexpected, and she notes that she had no sensory experience of the encounter aside from perceiving a distinct presence of love. Moreover, she trusted this experience, as she had never read any mystical works and therefore felt assured that she had not invented the encounter.

After these religious experiences, she came to think of Plato as a mystic, to view the *Iliad* in a Christian light, and to hear Christian resonances of the incarnate God in the *Bhagavad Gita*. She would eventually learn the Our Father in Greek and recite that regularly, especially during the time she worked eight-hour days in the vineyards of her farmer friend Gustave Thibon, attempting to internalize the plight of grape pickers. Such ecumenical and diverse Christian experiences reflect Weil's primary commitment to truth and intellectual honesty, which led her to some unexpected conclusions. Chief among these was her approach to the problem of evil.

The problem of evil

Weil recognized on a deep level the challenges that human suffering posed to religious faith as well as the ways in which religious organizations had attempted to whitewash or rationalize their own contributions to human misery under the guise of God's will. In fact, she wrote that there is only one thing that shakes her confidence in and love of God, and that is when she is 'in contact with the affliction of other people'. Her method, as always, was to attend honestly to these very real challenges: 'I think that with very important things we do not overcome our obstacles. We look at them fixedly for as long as is necessary until, if they are due to the powers of illusion, they disappear', she wrote. But obstacles like the problem of evil are not illusory. 'If we want to get over them before they have disappeared,' she continued, 'we are in danger of those phenomena of compensation', exchanging one religious-ethical problem for several more (WG 14). How, then, can affliction be explained within a religious worldview without making the proverbial deal with the devil? To understand her answer to this question requires first grasping her view of creation.

Weil believed that God's creation of the world was, like the crucifixion of Christ, an act of self-renunciation, or 'kenotic love'; God refused to be *all*, thereby giving rise to the existence of something other than and at a remove from Godself—i.e. the universe. This otherness constituting creation means that God has forfeited omnipotence such that 'God can only be present in creation under the form of absence' (N 419). The vacuum left in the wake of God's abdication is what Weil calls 'necessity', reflecting a rending of God's unity and pure goodness. Necessity, at an 'infinite distance' from the good, includes such things as natural laws, physical mechanisms and limitations, mortality, suffering, and human free will, along with the moral forces that stem from such freedom. Evil is therefore one by-product of necessity, an ironic testament to God's self-sacrificial love.

According to Weil, as a result of the essential distance between necessity and God, fundamentally, human freedom consists of two distinct possibilities for moral orientation in the world: dispose oneself towards the supernatural/God by longing for the good that God represents, or give oneself over to the forces of necessity, including our natural proclivity to centre on expanding the self and feeding its base desires. The orientation towards God means that one will consent to the suffering that accompanies loving in the void—acknowledging the felt absence of God—which Weil thought is the prerequisite to being truly attentive, just, and compassionate.

On the other hand, refusing to acknowledge the void left by God's withdrawal indicates a prioritization of self-defensiveness, which amounts to a refusal to love and an attachment to fantastical consolations and deflections. In this state, we imaginatively 'fill the void' by believing that we are the centre of the universe and can be entirely self-sufficient. But such beliefs are the result of giving ourselves over to the laws of necessity (or moral 'gravity'). Anything that follows from this orientation away from the supernatural and towards the self is automatic and no longer subject to the initial freedom; people in this state behave like things.

No matter the orientation we choose, we are consenting to some form of obedience, according to Weil—either obedience to God or to mechanical necessity. Consenting to God simultaneously entails a rejection of those self-promoting practices and commitments which preclude the recognition that we are incomplete and hungering for absolute good. We cannot, that is, content ourselves with wholesale, uncritical investment in the relative or partial goods of this world (like other persons, political institutions, or religious organizations) that can easily become idols, making us (falsely) believe that we lack nothing and are already in paradise.

In this sense, human affliction can be a gift to us, Weil thought, for it puts us into the direct and unavoidable awareness of the extreme distance of God and of our inherent need for good beyond this world. In fact, if one who is afflicted continues, against all odds, to love the good and receives no earthly compensation, they represent 'the intersection of creation and its Creator', like the intersection of the arms of the Cross, a site of extraordinary suffering and purity that is as close to God as is possible for humans. This is the manifest paradox in Weil's approach to the problem of evil: at the times when God/the good feels most absent in a human life, if love for the good remains undiluted, then God is perfectly present in that terrible void. As she explains:

> Pure goodness is not anywhere to be found in [this world]. Either God is not almighty or he is not absolutely good, or else he does not command everywhere where he has the power to do so. Thus, the very existence of evil here below, far from disproving the reality of God, is the very thing that reveals him in his truth. (WG 89)

From this we see that Weil clearly prioritized belief in God's absolute goodness over a notion of an interventionist God who would assert their will at all times and places. In permitting the existence of things distinct from Godself, God's creative act was an act of love—that is, a demonstration of restraint and self-renunciation rather than one of self-expansion and control.

In response to this creative act of God's self-renunciation, Weil tells us that we should echo this gesture via something she terms 'decreation'. Decreation is also an act of loving self-renunciation to give priority to the existence of the suffering world and the good outside it, beyond our own wills and selfish desires. As a result of

God's withdrawal, humans have been given a strong sense of independence and self-sufficiency, but this sense is what must be returned to God in the decreative act—a move which also prevents us from contributing to evil and affliction in the world. In this way, our imitation of God (through emptying ourselves of our egoic tendencies) can also be understood as co-creation of a better, and more beautiful, world:

> An imaginary divinity has been given to man so that he may strip himself of it like Christ did of his real divinity. Renunciation. Imitation of God's renunciation in creation. In a sense, God renounces being everything. We should renounce being something. That is our only good.... We participate in the creation of the world by decreating ourselves. (GG 33)

Other religious inspirations

In the absence of a decreative spirit, religious organizations and creeds frequently become idols conjuring false paradises, according to Weil, by offering their adherents self-serving consolations, like the belief in an afterlife, or the sense that God is continually pleased with them. The religious organization itself can be a source of collective enthusiasms, blind loyalties, and simplistic 'us versus them' narratives that function to promote the individual egos which rally around it. Not surprisingly, then, Weil sees her own potential inclusion in the Catholic Church as not only something which is inconsistent with her sense of God's will to remain outside it, but also as a dangerous temptation that could falsely satiate her hunger for the absolute good. As she described to Father Perrin:

> Social enthusiasms have such power today, they raise people so effectively to the supreme degree of heroism in suffering and death, that I think it is as well that a few sheep should remain outside the fold in order to bear witness that the love of Christ is essentially something different. (WG 36)

For her, this self-imposed exile was not only part of her decreative project, but also an opportunity to mix with the masses of people inspired by other religious traditions and belief systems and to learn from them.

Weil was already receptive to insights of traditions like Taoism, Hinduism, and Buddhism, and various elements from these and other religious frameworks show up regularly in her writings. She was intensely interested in other cultures and expended significant energy in learning languages such as ancient Greek and Sanskrit so that she could read sacred texts in the original. She even affirmed the truth claims of traditions, even if her way of doing so was often to profess these truths when they happened to align with certain Christian ideas. In her 1942 *Letter to a Priest* (the priest being Father Marie-Alain Couturier), Weil argued that a number of lessons drawn from mythology, folklore, and other religions could be translated into Christian truths without distorting them:

> Every time that a man has, with a pure heart, called upon Osiris, Dionysus, Krishna, Buddha, the Tao, etc., the Son of God has answered him by sending the Holy Spirit. And the Holy Spirit has acted upon his soul, not by inciting him to abandon his religious tradition, but by bestowing upon him light...in the heart of that same religious tradition.   (LP 29)

Thus, Weil does not regard belief in other religious traditions as an obstacle to Christianity; in fact, the latter can be enhanced by the illuminations from the former. Her mystical approach to Christianity led her to openly embrace mysticisms of the East as complementary. Later in her letter to Father Couturier, she wrote:

> In practice, mystics belonging to nearly all the religious traditions coincide to the extent that they can hardly be distinguished. They represent the truth of each of these traditions.

The contemplation practiced in India, Greece, China, etc., is just as supernatural as that of the Christian mystics. More particularly, there exists a very close affinity between Plato and, for example, St. John of the Cross. Also between the Hindu Upanishads and St. John of the Cross. Taoism, too, is very close to Christian mysticism.   (LP 47)

With respect to Taoism in particular, in her *Notebooks*, Weil cites the Taoist principle that one who possesses 'true virtue has not got any virtue'; that is, a truly virtuous person will be unconscious of any nobility of character they exude and would in fact deny that they are virtuous (N 20). Such a description coheres with her vision of a saint, who would essentially be anonymous to the world and not experience self-satisfaction over any good actions performed. She cites the Gospel story in which Christ told his disciples that when he was hungry, they gave him meat. 'When was that, Lord?' they had asked. Weil remarks that such ignorance is exemplary: 'We must not know when we do such acts' (N 358). Such an unselfconsciousness in our interactions with others is the sign of real generosity.

In other passages, she cites Taoist ideas about the non-acting action of effective work: 'Taoists: a good blacksmith does his work without thinking about it and doesn't tire himself' (N 112). Such an idea clearly influenced her conception of attention as she articulated it in *Reflections on the Right Use of School Studies with a View to the Love of God*. In this essay, she described attention as a 'negative effort' that should not involve tiredness. Furthermore, she wrote that to be attentive requires a suspension and detachment of our thought, so that our minds are completely open, empty, and ready to be penetrated by the realities we encounter—akin to the Taoist image of a mind as clear, receptive, and adaptable as water.

Weil was also influenced heavily by Hinduism, notably from her study of the *Upanishads* and *Bhagavad Gita*. For instance, she frequently cited the idea that we should be detached from the fruits of our actions, as was Arjuna's imperative in the *Gita*: 'Acting not *on behalf* of a certain object, but *as a result of* a certain necessity. I am unable to do otherwise. This is not action, but a sort of passivity' (N 124). Every action, according to Weil, should be considered from the point of view of its origin, not its aim, such that anything that is considered purely good will not come from the human will. This is religiosity for Weil: we should be receptive to and impelled by God in our actions. Acting without intention but out of a sense of necessity deriving from our full attention to another person (in whom God may be implicitly present) is essential for the practice of genuine compassion, in which the beneficiary does not feel indebted. This virtue is also illustrated in Weil's retelling of the Gospel parable of the Good Samaritan who, because of his attentiveness, stops to help the dirty, naked, and injured man on the roadside, automatically and almost in spite of himself.

Weil's ideas of detachment from desire, pure attention, emptiness of mind, the limitations of language, the impermanence of earthly attachments, and the relinquishment of illusions are likewise drawn directly from Buddhism: 'The idea behind Zen Buddhism: to perceive *purely*, without any admixture of reverie (my idea when I was seventeen)', she commented in her *Notebooks* (406). She compared meditation on contraries (which helps in perception of higher truths) to contemplation of the seemingly nonsensical Buddhist *koan*, like, *hear the sound of one hand clapping!* Searching for meaning in the *koan* produces a 'dark night which is followed by illumination', Weil says, indicating that its efficacy in halting our rational appropriations of the world is a precursor to genuine attention, holding a place for the higher mysteries which do not make sense to our limited intelligence. As Weil writes, 'The methods employed by the masters of Zen tend to carry the attention to the highest degree of intensity' (N 399).

Nor was Weil concerned with any projection of divinity upon a figure like the Buddha: 'If the anguished waiting for a Saviour led to a mistaken identification of the person known as Buddha with this saviour, and if he is invoked today as a perfect, divine man and redeemer, then this invocation is as efficacious as those addressed to Christ' (FLN 121). For Weil, the figure of the saviour is rooted in the role of a self-sacrificial mediator who serves as a bridge between the temporal and the transcendent. Both Christ and the Buddha had intimate knowledge of human suffering and transformed this experience into compassion and universal love for others—something Weil saw as indicative of holiness, bridging suffering with eternal peace.

In short, religious traditions which centred on divine renunciation or relinquishment of power had the kernel of truth that Weil sought and admired. She called these traditions the 'true religion', whereas the 'religions which represent divinity as commanding wherever it has the power to do so seem false' (WG 89). This latter statement is perhaps surprisingly indicative of Weil's controversial assessment of Judaism.

Judaism

As much as Weil was ecumenical in her incorporation of these Eastern religious insights into her Christian outlook, she was infamously unsympathetic (and even hostile at times) to Judaism, even neglecting Jewish mystical traditions which she would have likely esteemed highly. Weil scholars have regularly taken her to task for her narrow and ungenerous readings of Judaism and of the Tanakh. While such readings cannot be justified, it is worthwhile to consider her (sometimes flawed) thinking behind the harsh criticisms, as it illuminates what she finds valuable in other religious traditions.

In large part, her antipathy towards Judaism derives from both her assessment of the character of Jehovah, whom she views as a power-focused, jealous type of God, and her reading of Judaism as a 'national religion' appropriate only for empires (FLN 215). As

Weil sees it, Jehovah is an 'earthly god' that is the source of collectivist and exclusivist energies conducive to privileging a particular group of people ('the chosen') over and against others. In her writings, we come across statements such as: 'Jehovah made the same promises to Israel that the Devil made to Christ' (FLN 100); 'Jehovah the God of armies has conquered the whole world' (FLN 215); 'the Hebrews got the God they deserved: a carnal and collective God' (GG 159); 'Israel stood up to Rome because its God, even though immaterial, was a temporal sovereign on a par with the Emperor' (GG 161); and so on.

While some scholars have suggested that the source of these sentiments can be found in a psychological defect—that Weil is a self-hating Jew—there is a more likely philosophical explanation. The crux of Weil's criticisms of Judaism resides in what she sees as the religion's fixation on power in the absence of a mediator, like Christ, which checks and limits God's omnipotence via self-sacrificial love. 'Israel chose the national God and simultaneously rejected the Mediator', she wrote. In the absence of such an incarnate mediator, she believed that God could only be present to persons collectively, as 'the God of the tribe' (GG 160). If we recall Weil's denunciation of collectivities and religious patriotisms, it is not difficult to grasp her antipathy for a god-figure that promises to unite a people on the basis of conquering others.

Moreover, Weil reads idolatry as interwoven into the fabric of Judaism. She wrote to Father Couturier:

> The veritable idolatry is covetousness...and the Jewish nation, in its thirst for carnal good, was guilty of this in the very moments even when it was worshipping its God. The Hebrews took for their idol, not something made of metal or wood, but a race, a nation, something just as earthly. Their religion is essentially inseparable from such idolatry, because of the notion of the 'chosen people.' (LP 16)

Even though Weil is clearly guilty of making sweeping generalizations in this and other similar statements, she highlights a historical and theological point: the ancient Hebrews endorsed a theology that hypocritically denounced idol worship while they simultaneously erected for themselves a new idol—the nation of Israel.

The prohibition against idols in the form of images and material objects, like statues, does not prevent the elevation of a nation or a people in idolatrous fashion. Weil believed that Moses had banned idolatrous images 'so that Israel should continue to believe that its little national idol was God himself'; they would not have believed it, she contended, 'if the little idol had been a statue'. Whereas, according to her, Moses' aim was for the Hebrews to see 'their own collective soul [as] God' for the sake of Israel's temporal greatness, she suggested that, in contrast, Christ 'made God his only idol'. What is the difference here? According to Weil, the distinction is a significant one: 'to make God one's idol and to make one's idol God are two contrary movements. Just as there are two contrary conceptions of royalty: to make one's desires the law, or to make the law one's desire' (FLN 214). In short, her concern was that the God of the Jews had been (and continued to be) constructed out of earthly and collective desires such that this God had become a national fetish, to which they held exclusive and imperialist interests.

It is regrettable, of course, that Weil did not read more nuance, beauty, and goodness in the Jewish sacred texts and history, as she did with many other religious and mythical traditions. There is no religion that has not been tainted by its followers, no god that is not liable to collectivist passions or projections of selfish, power-hungry desires. She might have taken her own advice, as she put it in her letter to Father Couturier:

> The various authentic religious traditions are different reflections of the same truth, and perhaps equally precious. But we do not realize

this, because each of us lives only one of these traditions and sees the others from the outside. But...a religion can only be known from the inside.   (LP 34)

Grace, gravity, and atheism as purification

In general, when it came to religious organizations, rituals, experiences, and beliefs, Weil grasped both the intrinsic beauty and potential for meaningful, humbled existence that religions enshrine as well as the oppressions, exclusions, collective distractions, and self-righteous attitudes that are frequently the by-products of the same belief systems. Ever mindful of the ways in which religion has been used throughout history to justify evils like colonial violence, the suppression of thinking, and flights from present realities (in favour of imaginings of the afterlife), Weil was explicit about the dangers of religious authority and obedience—particularly for those who seek constant affirmations of the self and of base desires through religious belief.

Drawing inspiration from the Upanishads as much as from Plato, Weil thought that the human psyche comprised two basic capacities: a rational, truth-seeking, self-decentring capability and a thoughtlessly consumptive, self-seeking, reality-avoidant capacity. Throughout her writings, Weil referred to this duality in various ways. At times, she juxtaposed the capacities as 'looking' versus 'eating', the former clearly representing the religious-ethical approach in her philosophy, with the latter reflecting the root of evil:

> It may be that vice, depravity, and crime are nearly always, or even perhaps always, in their essence, attempts to eat beauty, to eat what we should only look at. Eve began it. If she caused humanity to be lost by eating the fruit, the opposite attitude, looking at the fruit without eating it, should be what is required to save it. 'Two winged companions,' says an Upanishad, 'two birds are on the branch of a tree. One eats the fruit, the other looks at it.' These two birds are the two parts of our soul.   (WG 105)

In other places, as we have seen, Weil poses this duality as our essential choice at every turn: to consent to the love of God, with the perpetual openness, attentiveness, and suffering that that entails, or to consent to the obedience of the material world, with the forces of power struggle, mechanical necessity, and greed that dictates therein. The former allows for the penetration of *grace* in the world, while the latter reflects the rule of *gravity*, according to Weil.

Grace is a gift from God, like illumination upon a dark landscape. It is grace that makes the imitation of God—also known as self-renunciation or decreation—possible for us, for drawing upon our human will alone would be insufficient to escape the natural pull of the ego. Grace is something alien to and unnatural within our world of mechanical necessity and selfishness; it is experienced as a miracle, or as the unexpected locus of radical transformation for what seems naturally impossible. Grace is also an interruption of force, which characterizes the material world ruled by moral gravity (that irresistible pull of the ego). Gravity, in this sense, is a 'downward' inclination towards human baseness, injustice, and evil—the creaturely nature in us that simply seeks to consume, expand, or to act with force towards obtaining our desires or deflecting our pains.

Religion itself can be approached in either of these two ways, like the fruit on the tree that can be looked at or eaten. While it is understandable that many people are attracted to religious belief and practice because, like food, it fills a natural desire for the person (like consolation or self-affirmation), such usage of religion is illegitimate and problematic in Weil's thinking. She tells us:

> Religion in so far as it is a source of consolation is a hindrance to true faith: in this sense atheism is a purification. I have to be atheistic with the part of myself which is not made for God. Among those men in whom the supernatural part has not been awakened, the atheists are right and the believers wrong. (N 238)

In other words, a person who is dictated by a consumptive, self-seeking demeanour in relation to religion—as evidenced by such things like self-righteousness, pride in religious roles or participation, using religion to diminish others, or selectively embracing religious doctrine to produce an irresponsible feel-good experience—should actually *renounce* that religion, for it has become one more element in the domain of moral gravity and necessity.

Religion, as we have seen, can be an idol and a void-filler, blocking the potential for grace and its reception. This tends to happen when we seek religion as some form of self-enhancement, salve, or power. For Weil, the antidote to this problematic appropriation of religion is to contemplate the difficult present realities and the resulting voids, without attempting to console or distract ourselves, and while maintaining a desire for goodness that cannot be found in the domain of gravity. False gods, idols, and collective enthusiasms can be easy to confuse with genuine religiosity, but they prevent access to the true God who resists objectification and fetishization, according to Weil. For this reason, true religiosity in Weil's philosophy appears as a kind of absurd paradox, a negative theology: we must consent to the supernatural, but that is precisely what we cannot affirm or grasp. 'We have to be in a desert,' Weil writes, 'for he whom we must love is absent.'

Chapter 5
Ethics

Simone Weil was always a philosopher of ethics, no matter the subject she was addressing at any given time. She had a heightened consciousness for matters of injustice, including the causes and effects of affliction in humans, and these concerns infused her writing and her actions alike. Her particular approach to moral questions reflected a new kind of ethical theory, one that appears to bring together divergent elements of Kantian deontology (duty-based ethics) and later contemporary care ethics, but which cannot be entirely framed by either of these. Like Kant, Weil highlighted the importance of impersonal, self-decentred obedience to a higher law, placing moral value on the kinds of actions that demonstrate respect for persons as dignified ends-in-themselves, in spite of our base inclinations to favour ourselves and grant ourselves moral exceptions.

In contrast, Weil might also be said to have anticipated the *moral orientation* focus of contemporary care ethics, particularly with her emphasis on the experiential significance of intersubjective attentiveness that manifests as a heightened capacity for appropriate responsiveness and compassion. Care ethicists—like Carol Gilligan, Nel Noddings, Virginia Held, and Marilyn Friedman—contend that attending to and meeting the needs of particular others we encounter, centring personal relationships and communal ties in moral decision-making, and highlighting connection, compassion, and deep listening as crucial qualities of moral engagement are necessary to temper the too-abstract and experientially detached frameworks of ethical theories like deontology and utilitarianism. There are, for instance, few universal rules that a care ethicist would adopt or endorse, and even notions like universal love would be at odds, for a care ethicist, with the specificity of particular, present relationships in our lives that we rightly privilege. While Weil describes the necessity of compassion towards others, especially those who are afflicted, she is clear that this attitude should derive from a detached and impersonal framework of self-renouncing love-as-justice, so that ego does not enter into the equation.

Thus, deriving from her religious-metaphysical views, Weil's ethical philosophy centres on the practice of attending to particular others *and* to the world at large. Recall that for her, there is essentially one moral choice presented to us at any given time. This is the choice between two basic orientations: we can consent to the forces of the natural world and be governed by mechanical necessity and the moral gravity it entails, or we can sincerely desire the (absent) good (or God), positioning ourselves to receive supernatural grace which answers the hunger for goodness. Only the latter can be characterized as attention; accordingly, our supernatural hunger for the good, which enables us to see that same, sacred hunger for goodness in another person, constitutes the foundation of the moral fabric of our beings.

These two dispositions also indicate differing relations to our selves. In orienting towards material values (and away from the supernatural), we centre the self and its base desires. Conversely, when we recognize the lack of pure goodness in our world and embrace our longing for something transcendent and truly good, we decentre the self and experience the void (*le vide*) that reflects our incomplete being in an imperfect world. That is, in becoming attentive, we are not only able to see what is external to us, in all its reality, but we are also able to know the reality of ourselves: our mediocrity, our finitude, and our vulnerability to moral gravity, and, finally, our nothingness in the sense of the void. To fully appreciate Weil's ethical philosophy requires unpacking her notion of the void and its relation to the self. This analysis in turn illuminates her conception of evil and its relation to illusion, as well as her understanding of goodness and its connection to attentiveness. Finally, Weil's description of a certain kind of moral education gives us a pragmatic avenue for engaging in the cultivation of attention.

The void and the self

As we have seen, in Weil's account of the creation of the world, God's refusal to be everything constitutes the creation of *something else*—the universe and all it contains. The kenotic act of love in God's creation also means that what is not-God (the created) is characterized by an incompleteness or vacuum, left in the wake of God's withdrawal. This vacuum extends to our own being; according to Weil, humans comprise an internal void (*le vide*), a lacking that is often experienced as existential hunger, emotional disequilibrium, the 'dark night of the soul', or the raw feeling of bottomless despair as when a loss or tragedy occurs.

While this void is an integral part of each individual's being, we often do not recognize it, by design, for we also have been created with a sense of self that is allergic to the void and sees it as a threat. Weil tells us that, as part of our human condition, the sense of self, that 'imaginary royalty', generally tries to conceal, placate, or fill the void, denying its reality while asserting a fabricated sense of wholeness, self-sufficiency, and greatness. That is, in response to the experience of the void, the self exerts a gravitational-like pull upon objects, pursuits, and ideas that would (at least temporarily) provide a reassurance against the threat of our own mediocrity and mortality. People can hardly tolerate the void, for it is a constant reminder of our limitations and losses in the world. Thus, the self constructs consoling narratives, seeks out distractions, consumes (food, commodities, relationships, narcotics), reacts defensively and sometimes violently towards anything/anyone that would expose its basis, and most significantly, denies its own essential hunger for the good—all for the sake of avoiding the pain that accompanies this constitutive emptiness.

Weil often refers to the self as 'the I' (*le moi*)—a gift from God that is meant to be returned through the process of decreation, the ethical response to our created nature:

> We possess nothing in the world—a mere chance can strip us of everything—except the power to say 'I'. That is what we have to give to God—in other words, to destroy. There is absolutely no other free act which it is given us to accomplish—only the destruction of the 'I'. (N 336)

To love truth means to endure the void and to appreciate the distance between ourselves and the good: to consent to decreation and ultimately, to accept death. Few are capable of truly doing this, Weil thought, and even then, acceptance of the void tends to happen in brief moments 'when everything stands still, instants of contemplation, or pure intuition'.

Most of the time, however, we devote ourselves to an order that has at its centre either ourselves or some other being/collective—like a partner, a political figure, an ideology, or an imagined god—with which we have identified ourselves. Self-absorption and self-expansion via identification are primary modes of void-filling. When one centres on the self in either of these ways, it is the *imaginary or false idea of a reified self that is the object of fixation*. Our true being (mediocre, limited, mortal—in short, the void) inspires fear and disgust, so we avoid this truth at all costs. As a result, we create narratives to assure ourselves of our sufficiency and greatness, which exclude the actual contingencies, humiliations, and gaps comprising our beings. Many people even begin to believe their own fictions. Weil employs an eloquent metaphor to capture this condition:

> A painter doesn't draw the place where he himself is. But looking at his painting, I know his position in relation to the things he has drawn. On the contrary, if he represents himself in his painting, I know with certainty that the place he shows himself to be isn't the one where he is. (FLN 146)

In other words, if we make ourselves the object of our focus, we will of necessity represent ourselves (to us and to others) wrongly—like a filtered and staged selfie. On the other hand, we present ourselves most truthfully when we have forgotten about ourselves through attentiveness to the world beyond. This reflection of attention that results in lucid self-*awareness* is distinct from a void-filling self-*preoccupation*. At the same time that the self is revealed as inherently humbled when we refuse to conceal the void, a definitive ethical posture arises from this renunciation, self-emptying, and openness—an ethics of attention. However, the temptation to negate the void is ever-present and overwhelming, and it is also the source of evil and illusion.

Evil and illusion

When we experience pain, whether physical or mental, our focus is drawn to the injury and an automatic defensive reaction is triggered that typically involves some kind of consolation or compensation for the felt harm. Oftentimes, such compensations are found in forms of escapism when no other relief is available—like fantasies or metanarratives that purport to justify and redeem the suffering (e.g. 'this tragedy was willed by God'). But as much as these projections may function as a salve for the wounded, Weil perceives a dark and dangerous aspect to these natural reactions. In a letter to Joë Bousquet, a French poet and quadriplegic whose spine was shattered in the First World War and who was living bedridden in Dourgne in 1942, Weil wrote:

> I believe that the root of evil, in everybody perhaps, but certainly in those whom affliction has touched...is day-dreaming. It is the sole consolation, the unique resource of the afflicted; the one solace to help them bear the fearful burden of time; and a very innocent one, besides being indispensable. So how could it be possible to renounce it? It has only one disadvantage, which is that it is unreal.
>
> (SL 139)

For Weil, this statement was a challenging and radical claim concerning the nature and source of evil. In her philosophy, evil derives from the unrealities produced by the void-filling imagination, the seeking of 'equilibrium' through illusion, and its inherent deflections of suffering.

In this sense, evil, contrary to the manner in which it is presented by the media and entertainment industries, is literally *nothing new*, since it always stems from our impoverished attempts to rectify our mortal incompleteness. 'Evil is license and that is why it is monotonous: everything has to be drawn from ourselves', Weil explains (N 183). Because it is not given to humans to create except through decreation, evil is 'a bad attempt to imitate God'. Any such attempt, then, to negate the void reveals the perpetrator acting in the realm of the imaginary: s/he acts to obtain something that is illusory (for void-filling is temporary, at best). Therefore, while fictitious evil is romantic and varied, real evil is actually 'gloomy, monotonous, barren, boring'; its root is perpetually the fabrications of the limited self (N 192).

Ironically, however, the self tends to *experience* evil as such only when the void is maintained and consolations are bracketed: 'We experience evil only by refusing to allow ourselves to do it, or, if we do it, by repenting of it. When we do evil we do not know it, because evil flies from the light' (GG 71). Evil experienced by an innocent person is suffering, while evil done is a response of moral gravity providing cover to an insatiable ego. 'That which is not felt by the criminal is his own crime', Weil writes, adding: 'That which is not felt by the innocent victim is his own innocence' (GG 72). In pure or 'innocent' beings, unjust attacks and violence are transmuted into suffering since there is no outward transference of the energy (like in revenge) to establish moral equilibrium. But in communicating and displacing our suffering onto the world, we contribute to a contagious spread of evil in which others pay the price of our avoidance and degradation. Meanwhile, the evildoer has a (false) sense of deliverance.

When 'the I' is intent upon its own protection and refusal of the void, it leaves its mark on the world in a destructive fashion. In succumbing to the orientation of comfort and pleasure, that is, we leave new blemishes on the world. We become increasingly banal, and genuine attention to those who are afflicted becomes more and more difficult the more we a-void (negate our void). In such cases, we enter into a vicious downward spiral of self-gratification and multiplication of evil via those upon whom we unload our grievances. As Weil admitted, when she had a headache, the temptation to strike another person in that exact part of their head was nearly irresistible. And were that to happen, that victim would then be tempted to communicate their suffering to a third person, and so on. Only by absorbing and halting the natural reactionary processes spurred by harm to us can we slow the spread of evil. The void, in other words, is what makes evil so predictable, but it is also the site of a potentially miraculous transmutation of crime into suffering, of evil into innocence.

The good and attention

Given the preceding discussion, it should be clear that for Weil, true goodness implies attention to and through the experience of the void that is our reality. In fact, anything that confers greater openness and insight into reality is good, according to Weil. This is why attentiveness that corresponds with self-abdication is so highly valued in her ethical philosophy; by orienting ourselves towards the world as it is, setting aside comforting distractions,

8. Simone Weil at a café with Jean Lambert, André Gide's son-in-law, 1941.

fictions, and denials, not only are we more in touch with the actual needs of the world, but we also preserve the possibility for others to grasp reality through our decreated being.

Goodness therefore arises in humans via attention which is a subtraction of our egos—getting out of the way so that we do not obscure *what is* from the perspective of others. Another way of thinking about this process, in religious terms, is that we should become like invisible mediators between the Creator and creation, so that contact with truth may be readily made. Weil describes this process:

> It is possible for us to be mediators between God and the part of creation which is confided to us. Our consent is necessary in order that he may perceive his own creation through us.... God can love in us only this consent to withdraw in order to make way for him, just as he himself, our creator, withdrew in order that we might come into being. (GG 41)

Goodness, then, is not found in assertive or intentional 'good deeds', but rather through negation of our natural tendencies to centre the self. By emptying ourselves of our own desires to be *seen as good*, we become vehicles for the truth to penetrate situations in which we are involved, thus fostering the good. Though goodness cannot be willed, because it comes from outside us, it clearly requires an extraordinary amount of (negative) effort and patience. For Weil, 'negative effort' in attending is characterized by a relaxation of the seeking, grasping, and willing energies, supplanting them with an opening of perspective and detachment from self-interested aims. Negative effort here is also subtractive in nature, like the effort required to wipe a dirty pane of glass clean so that more of the horizon comes into our field of vision.

As we have seen, evil derives from the assertions and interferences of the self and is therefore constrained to be unoriginal and banal. On the other hand, true goodness, in completely eluding the will and being done almost in spite of ourselves, is unexpected, novel, and, therefore, immensely interesting. Weil gives an example:

> A man coming down a ladder, who misses a step and falls, is either a sad or an uninteresting sight, even the first time we see it. But if a man were walking in the sky as though it were a ladder, going up into the clouds and coming down again, he could do it every hour of every day and we would never be tired of watching. It is the same with pure good; for a necessity as strong as gravity condemns man to evil and forbids him any good.   (SNL 160)

Gravity (physical and moral) is, in other words, natural and expected. But the overcoming of this gravity is compelling. For Weil, such goodness is not merely the opposite of evil, for this would put them on the same (natural) level. Instead, she tells us that good is essentially *other than* evil:

> That which is the direct opposite of an evil never belongs to the order of higher good. It is often scarcely any higher than evil!

Examples: theft and the bourgeois respect for property; adultery
and the 'respectable woman; the savings bank and waste; lying and
'sincerity'.   (N 127)

These so-called 'goods' like respect for property, the savings bank,
and sincerity are forms of what Weil calls 'degraded good'.
However, such 'degraded good' is capable of being corrupted by
evil, and, not surprisingly, degraded good is more difficult to
recognize and resist than evil, perhaps because prestige
accompanies the former. We must renounce it just as we must
renounce ordinary evil.

Real goodness, on the other hand, is 'an unfathomable marvel'
that is too often desecrated at the hands of writers and artists
who render it unremarkable and evil fascinating. We 'envelop
[the truth of the good] in a fog in which, as in all fiction, values
are reversed, so that evil is attractive and good is tedious', when in
fact, 'nothing is so beautiful and wonderful, nothing is so
continually fresh and surprising, so full of sweet and perpetual
ecstasy, as the good' (SNL 162, 160). Again, this is because the
manifestations of baseness are finite, for they issue from finite
creatures.

Thus, if we are to create something that could be called 'beautiful'
or 'good', we must take on the transparency of the proverbial
window pane to allow the light of supernatural values (from
outside us) to shine through. In a similar vein, when we have
genuine love for our neighbours, which is a supernatural love
passing through us, we affirm them as unique beings and grant
them the attentive silence that is rightfully theirs, permitting their
reality to penetrate us. When we succumb to degraded forms of
good, however, 'we do not study other people; we invent what they
are thinking, saying, and doing' (SNL 161). That is, when we do
not preserve an interior void that is the condition for
attentiveness, we project onto people what we wish to hear and
see from them; we fabricate who they are, effectively precluding

any real relationship, or love. Love, Weil reminds us, 'needs reality'.

Love is therefore not self-consoling. It does not protect us from being wounded or feeling the pain of the world; on the contrary, it is defined by its vulnerability and defencelessness in the face of crushing realities. However, Weil also suggests that love is *creative*, in that it sees what tends to be marginalized and obscured by a society intent on a sanitized, feel-good appearance. The parable of the Good Samaritan epitomizes this kind of creative love for Weil:

> Love for our neighbor, being made of creative attention, is analogous to genius. Creative attention means really giving our attention to what does not exist. Humanity does not exist in the anonymous flesh lying inert by the roadside. The Samaritan who stops and looks gives his attention all the same to this absent humanity, and the actions which follow prove that it is a question of real attention. (WG 92)

On the level of attention that can 'look' at affliction (having been prepared by solitude and exercises of self-effacement), love is truly made possible. Creative attention, which is really a decreation, allows us to be transported *into* the experience of the afflicted other, rather than the reverse which is caused by the self-protective imagination: distorting the experience and being of the other to conform to my self-interested perspective. Thus, loving and attending to the other means that we accept diminishment of our egos, for it is a necessary consequence any time we are truly open to the reality of other persons. Defined in this way, love is not supererogatory for Weil; it is a necessary condition for being ethical and just.

In this loving, we also detach ourselves from any possible return from the being we love. There are no strings attached. According to Weil, loving someone means being able to ask them, *What are you going through?* 'It is a recognition the sufferer exists', she contends, 'as a man, exactly like us, who was one day stamped with a special mark by affliction' (WG 64). In other words, to love is to embrace the void/hunger of another without explaining it away and without forgetting one's own hunger for the good. If love needs reality, then it arises from and fixes on the void, whether our own or that of another person. As attention and decreation are inextricably joined together, our attentiveness makes it more likely that others will see reality as well. In the transparency that attention manifests, we not only become an impartial reader of reality, but we also cease to be the obscurity (which having an assertive personal perspective brings) that serves as a distraction to other beings.

Certain actions are automatic and others are prevented by the mere practice of attending. When giving attention to someone who is hungry, for instance, we will be unable to resist feeding them, and it will be impossible to laugh at their plight. But the unselfconsciousness that characterizes genuine attention also means that we are not aware of our good deeds as such; we are simply the vehicle that understands that the source of love is external to us. Since any goodness follows from a consent to the void, one's disposition and ensuing actions can never generate pride. Instead, our obedience would be characterized by 'fear and trembling', to use Kierkegaard's phrase. As Weil explains,

> Good which is done in this way, almost in spite of ourselves, almost shamefacedly and apologetically, is pure. All absolutely pure goodness completely eludes the will. Goodness is transcendent...
> 'I was an hungered, and ye gave me meat.' When was that, Lord? They did not know. We must not know when we do such acts. We must not help our neighbor *for* Christ but *in* Christ. May the self disappear in such a way that Christ can help our neighbor through the medium of our soul and body. (GG 45–6)

It should be clear that Weil's notion of attentiveness indicates an orientation away from and beyond the self, just as she suggested that real, transcendent energy (grace) comes from outside ourselves and cannot be the result of our own seeking. 'Attention alone—that attention which is so full that the "I" disappears—is required of me. I have to deprive all that I call "I" of the light of my attention and turn it on to that which cannot be conceived' (N 179). Attention is an orientation which reveals to us not only our own limitations, but also the afflictions, imposed silences, marginalized populations, inexpressible experiences, abject circumstances, hidden beauties, natural wonders, subtle gestures, overlooked assistants, infinitesimal details, and nuances of life, which are neglected in our typical self-centred states. How do we develop this seemingly miraculous and unnatural capacity, according to Weil?

Moral education

In her short but famous essay, 'Reflections on the Right Use of School Studies with a View to the Love of God', Weil outlines the way in which formal education, if approached in a particular manner, could be the basis for developing the capacity of moral attention. In fact, she contends that cultivating attentiveness *should* be the sole object of schooling.

Of course, Weil understood that there are different ways of educating, and many of these methods are more conducive to generating self-centredness, pride, and distractedness than actual attention. Education, which concerns itself with the motives for effective action, requires energy for the execution of study. The question is: What sort of energy will be sought and supplied for learning—the energy that comes from base motives connected to relative goods (like a higher grade point average, teachers' praise, a diploma, a job, material rewards), or the energy that Weil calls 'supernatural', which increases the hunger for the good, and preserves the inner void to stimulate attention to the world?

The type of energy that is supplied for educational pursuits will determine the kind of character and capacities being developed. We may wish to direct students towards the good by didactically teaching and prescribing certain values or by promising various rewards, but Weil argues that without the necessary motives, it is 'as if one tried, by pressing down on the accelerator, to set off in a motor-car with an empty petrol tank' (NR 188). Instead, educators must take care to disconnect the praxis of learning from the incentives of instant gratification, helping students to appreciate other, less tangible and more enduring goods along the way.

Patience is key and constitutes a necessity for strengthening a student's capacity for supernatural attention; in fact, in Weil's description, patience is practically synonymous with attention. The French word *l'attention* (like its English translation) derives from the Latin *attendere*, 'to stretch towards', which also gave us the French verb, *attendre*, 'to wait'. Importantly, Weil thought the most precious gifts in life (whether in academics, or in spiritual matters) are obtained by 'waiting for them', stretching towards the good with a receptive, curious, and open mind. Conversely, she thought that all intellectual errors are made by 'the fact that thought has seized upon some idea too hastily, and being thus prematurely blocked, is not open to the truth' (WG 62). Students frequently attach to ideas or solutions unthinkingly in a rush to get done with work, but haste and the distaste for the slower *process of learning* are only conducive to void-filling, self-contented, and distracted tendencies.

It is true that Weil writes of school studies as cultivating a 'lower kind of attention' (compared to a higher form of attention such as found in prayer); at first glance, this seems to denigrate attention in educational contexts as not worthy of our time or investment. Yet lower kinds of attention only signify that the objects of such attention are more or less approximate to the good; but their lowered status does not entail distractedness or idolatry, as long as we recognize their distance from the absolute (i.e. their relative nature). For example, geometry may not be equivalent to the good, but approaching geometric problems with a sincere desire to grasp their meaning, coherence with reality, and solutions can be a model for more profound instances of patient attending. Moreover, intellectual exercises are valuable insofar as we learn difficult truths about ourselves—namely, truths about our intellectual limitations, our mediocrity, and the void that constitutes us.

Likewise, Weil thinks that the capacity for attention is present in every person's being, as each of us is naturally humbled, being at a distance from perfection. It is an orientation we are capable of choosing, if only we are willing to recognize and face the void. She makes this point clear when she says, 'We do not have to acquire humility. There is humility in us. Only we humiliate ourselves before false gods' (N 274). We know this humility through experiences of shortcomings, failures, and errors in school—but again, we try to forget these truths.

Therefore, a reliable remedy for recollecting the truth about ourselves is to be found in school studies: 'When we force ourselves to fix the gaze, not only of our eyes, but of our souls, upon a school exercise in which we have failed through sheer stupidity, a sense of mediocrity is borne in upon us with irresistible evidence.' She continues, 'No knowledge is more to be desired. If we can arrive at knowing this truth with all our souls we shall be well established on the right foundation' (WG 60). In this approach to education, it matters little whether a student arrives at the right answers reliably or quickly, or whether they are proficient in a subject. The important thing for the cultivation of attention is the process of learning itself:

> If we have no aptitude or natural taste for geometry, this does not
> mean that our faculty for attention will not be developed by
> wrestling with a problem or studying a theorem. On the contrary, it
> is almost an advantage. It does not even matter much whether we

succeed in finding the solution or understanding the proof, although it is important to try really hard to do so. Never in any case whatever is a genuine effort of the attention wasted. It always has its effect on the spiritual plane and in consequence on the lower one of the intelligence, for all spiritual light lightens the mind. (WG 58)

For Weil, academic work approached in this way is so valuable that it would be worthwhile to sell all of our earthly possessions in order to be able to pursue it. Ultimately, this purely intellectual level of attention is a foundation for a more profound emotional and spiritual practice of attention that can be given over to other persons in times of crisis and need, manifesting needed compassion.

This ethics of attention bridges *caritas* with the strict obligations of justice. In fact, taking inspiration from the Gospels, Weil argues that we should not even distinguish between love of neighbour and the duty of justice: 'We have invented the distinction between justice and charity', she writes. We have done this, she explains, to relieve ourselves from the obligation of generosity under our narrower vision of justice as an exacting (re-)establishment of equilibrium. But true, supernaturally inspired justice mandates our loving attention—a gift—to the most downtrodden and marginalized among us. By the identification of compassion and justice, the spirit of care will not devolve into an obscene gratuitousness or self-interested charity, and just treatment will not be a calculating, inhuman exercise: 'Only the absolute identification of justice and love makes the coexistence possible of compassion and gratitude on the one hand, and on the other, of respect for the dignity of affliction in the afflicted—a respect felt by the sufferer himself and the others' (WG 85).

At its highest potential, such attention will result in prayer, according to Weil. But to be clear: prayer, understood in this way, is not the recitation of a wish list to God, nor is it an opportunity for self-affirmations or consolations. Prayer in the Weilian sense is the ultimate ethical posture: it is an unrelenting desire for and complete openness to the good that will in turn reconcile us with the void in ourselves and others. Our social mechanisms, institutions, and ideologies work to deny and conceal this essential hunger for the good, but the attentive person will recognize, as Weil did: 'Love sees what is invisible' (WG 92).

Chapter 6
Beauty

Attention is the ethical posture for Weil, but it is also an aesthetic orientation, for beauty sparks the initial dawning and development of the attention. Since the absent God/the good cannot be directly apprehended by us, our attention lands, of necessity, on the things of this world. Yet as we have seen, our attentiveness is constituted by a hunger for the eternal and the true, so there is a simultaneous attraction to and restlessness with earthly beauty—whether that be the natural world, persons, or the various objects of human artistry—insofar as they conceal and partially reveal true beauty. Weil calls these objects of our direct attention and love *metaxu*, a word which conveys their status as intermediaries between our longing for the eternal and the good/ beautiful itself.

Following a more detailed account of Weil's idea of metaxu, this chapter examines two categories of earthly beauty—art and nature—and what they reveal about Weil's aesthetic theory, as well as the kind of attentive disposition that is cultivated via encounters with such beauty.

Metaxu

There is for Weil a paradox concerning the world in which we live: it is both a 'closed door', or a separation from God (read: truth, genuine beauty, and the good), while also being a link to the absolute (N 492). The things of this world, that is, represent intermediaries, or metaxu, between humans and the divine; they serve as a veil to what is eternal but simultaneously are a bridge to God. For this reason, Weil thought that metaxu should be considered as earthly blessings, as our temporal means to something much greater. Our metaxu might consist of our home, traditions, pets, cultural artefacts, works of art, community, and natural environment among other things. Like us, these are within the domain of 'relative and mixed blessings...which warm and nourish the soul and without which, short of sainthood, a *human life* is not possible' (GG 147). Although this is the created world with an absent creator, it would be a crime and sacrilege to destroy any of these bridges linking the natural to the supernatural.

Since 'every separation is a link', according to Weil, as long as we are able to perceive the limited and relative nature of metaxu and love them as such, we can be delivered through the barrier to encounter what is transcendent. Weil uses the example of two prisoners who communicate with one another by knocking on the wall that separates them; it is their means of communication even though it is clearly an obstacle to their direct encounter. Pain also functions as metaxu in a similar sense: it registers as a physical limitation or restriction, but it is also what puts us in touch with the truth of ourselves—our mortal and vulnerable flesh, an expression of the void. It often takes an injury or disease for us to gain proper perspective on our desires and the values that animate them. Weil perceived the linkage between pain and beauty, as metaxu, on a deeply personal level, disclosing in her notebooks that she often felt her most poetic inclinations following her worst migraines (N 318).

Sensibly beautiful objects (or persons) are the most enticing forms of metaxu, and these have a unique function in Weil's thought. Drawing on Kantian aesthetic philosophy, beauty, Weil surmised, is 'the only finality here below', the only thing that is not a means to anything else (WG 105). At first glance, this would seem to indicate that beautiful manifestations cannot be metaxu, since the latter are defined by their intermediary nature. However, anything we rightly call 'beautiful' is that which contains a kernel of the divine and universal beauty; this is the sense in which the beautiful represents an end in itself. But beautiful objects or people also have an effect on our sensual, earthly nature and are especially effective in attracting our attention, eventually culminating in supernatural love for the good. Beauty arouses the desire and energy for pursuing the good, so it is a bridge, but it is one that must also be revered for its own sake. Weil explains this paradox:

> Nevertheless, as [beauty] is the only finality, it is present in all human pursuits. Although they are all concerned with means, for everything that exists here below is only a means, beauty sheds a luster upon them which colors them with finality. Otherwise there could neither be desire, nor, in consequence, energy in the pursuit. (WG 106)

Beauty is that initial spark which entreats us onto the path of lifelong education, or committed engagement with the world, and the corresponding expansion of our attention. Weil suggests that the bonds of ignorance and falsehood, represented in Plato's allegory of the cave by the chains keeping the prisoners fixed in their myopic and illusory perspectives, can be broken by 'the shock received from beauty' (SNL 123). A beautiful appearance is the most likely gateway to spur us on the journey out of the proverbial cave, towards knowledge, wisdom, and eternal truth. The caveat here is that it is important not to fixate and settle on the beautiful object as if it itself were absolute and pure, just as it is necessary not to disregard, denigrate, or bypass it in an otherworldly attempt to reach the divine: 'All these secondary kinds of beauty are of infinite value as openings to universal beauty', Weil writes (WG 104). With this recognition, we can come to see glimmers of beauty in varying degrees and across all manner of sensible objects that have the potential to open us to broader, more impersonal, and therefore universal truths.

There are, however, 'seductive factors' which can be easily confused with aspects of genuine beauty when they are present, especially due to lack of discernment. These factors tend to evoke our basest desires—desires for immediate gratification, appropriation of otherness, selfishness, and greed. Meanwhile, the characteristics of *real* beauty as identified by Weil—which will be detailed in the sections below—can arrest our tendencies to thoughtlessly consume and unjustly annex those objects, even as these elements of beauty appeal to our senses.

'Beauty', Weil explains, 'exerts a charm over the flesh in order to obtain permission to penetrate right to the soul' (N 317). There is always a risk of corruption involved in sensory attraction, given the similarity in some cases between degraded apparitions of beauty and real instances of it. But without the attraction of the body, there is no possibility for authentic inspiration or the cultivation of the attention to behold and contemplate reality. Beauty, as metaxu, is what harmonizes the precarity of our sensuous world with the eternal good. It is not so much an attribute of matter, Weil says, as it is 'a relationship of the world to our sensibility' (WG 103). It functions to attract us carnally and wholly while keeping us at a reverent, ethical-aesthetic distance.

The eternal in art

When it comes to human artefacts and works that could be considered 'beautiful' through a Weilian lens, there are a few important criteria to remember: beauty is a union of the sense of necessity with its roots in the sensible world, while being in obedience to the good; the beautiful attracts our notice but prompts our self-renouncing contemplation; finally, the beautiful enshrines the real presence of the divine in matter. In short, a beautiful work of art reflects the necessary and real conditions of human life brought on by the gravity of this world, while being like an incarnation of God, revealing elements of eternity; for beauty is a child of the earth and sky, natural and supernatural. This is why the beautiful work of art can be contemplated, but not easily fetishized, for the supernatural element cannot be objectified or possessed, according to Weil. On the contrary, though, *we* can be possessed and captured by beauty and brought to stillness and speechlessness.

The beautiful work of art provides no ultimate consummation but is an attraction that pushes back against our egoistic projections. When real beauty has infused or inspired the art object of our attraction, it compels respect and a self-abnegating beholding of the beautiful: 'To *respect* the thing that one desires—this is the source of piety, of art, of contemplation...Platonism', she writes (FLN 52). What epitomizes beautiful art from this perspective? Weil's examples of beautiful works are not surprising, given her primary inspirations and philosophy: Sophocles' *Antigone*, the Christian Gospels, Gregorian chants, Bach's concertos, and Greek statues. Weil sees that certain objects such as these, in their transcendent beauty, have an ennobling effect upon the psyches of the beholders and remind us of what we lack—pure, unadulterated goodness, harmony, and justice.

To employ another example, from her lectures we find: 'Architecture: a child, as a matter of instinct, does not play around in a cathedral', for 'what is beautiful takes hold of the body' (LOP 184). This statement suggests the unlikelihood of distractedness—even for a child—in the presence of a work that inspires awe and compels silence, stillness, contemplation. Like a moral exemplar, the cathedral has a concrete and transformative effect on those who would attend to it. The same could be said of the Greek statues, Gregorian chants, and *Antigone*. Weil tells us that beauty 'teaches us that mind can come down into nature...Beauty is a witness that the ideal can become a reality' (LOP 189). The ideal only becomes incarnate when the artist is supernaturally attentive, however. The artist should have the same disposition as one who is truly compassionate or just: empty of self-regard, open to reality, courageous in facing the inner void, patient, quiet, listening, and consenting to be a vehicle for inspiration and grace exceeding our natural tendencies and talents. Only in this way can a merely talented artist become a genius, Weil tells us, yet the beautiful work transcends even the genius, who is merely the vehicle for this incarnation of the divine: 'A work of art has an author and yet, when it is perfect, there is something essentially anonymous about it. It imitates the anonymity of divine art' (N 241).

It is for this reason that the beautiful work of art can be wholly contemplated without restlessness or distraction. According to Weil, we can really fix our attention on the beautiful, gazing or listening for hours on end. 'Gregorian music. When the same things are sung for hours each day and every day, whatever falls even slightly short of supreme excellence becomes unendurable and is eliminated' (N 81). Although for many people, the thought of listening to Gregorian chants for hours conjures an image of monotony and boredom, Weil believed that art forms which are impersonal, universal, and balanced (like the ancient Greek values of symmetry and harmony), with only the most essential notes, words, or images, do not conduce to fatigue, but instead feed our desire for what is eternal and keep us returning. Conversely, one does grow tired of what is merely pleasing, that which 'only flatters the senses', Weil contends (LOP 184). Like a hit pop song, or the latest fashion trend reflecting a zeitgeist, such attractions can entertain us for a limited amount of time, but their discrete timeliness and relative superficiality mean that there is little to compel us after the moment has passed.

The more impersonal an artwork is, the less the egoic personality of the artist appears in it and the more likely it is to be universal, timeless, and a work of genius that can convey supernatural values. In medieval Byzantine iconography such as 'Christ the

Pantocrator', expressionism and even expressions in the sacred face were discouraged due to their potential for arresting the observer at the superficial level of the representation and thus leading to idolatry (see Figure 9). The icons themselves were to be 'anonymous', and the artists were to refrain from investing their personalities in them or even signing them. As philosopher Richard Kearney explains, 'The common practice of portraying the eyes of Christ as expressionless was an apt symbol of the icon's primary function: to invite the onlooker to travel through the vacant regard of the image towards the suprasensible transcendence of God.'

Moreover, impersonality, Weil suggests, is what allows beauty to really 'cry out' and speak to us. Such speaking is a critical function of genuine art, for between beauty, truth, and justice, only beauty has a voice: '[Beauty] cries out and points to truth and justice who are dumb, like a dog who barks to bring people to his master lying unconscious in the snow', Weil writes (ANTH 73). Impersonality is efficacious in this way because it is also what is sacred, universal, and perfect in each human being: it is what connects us to the rest of humanity and does not reflect a purely personal interest. It constitutes the difference between seeing our proper place in the universe and thinking that we are the centre of it. With the latter disposition, our creations may be dazzling achievements that bring temporal fame, but 'above this level, far above, separated by an abyss, is the level where the highest things are achieved'—and those works feel essentially anonymous (ANTH 55).

Although this impersonal art of the genius is imbued with divine inspiration and hence has a morally elevating potential, there is simultaneously contact with the truth of moral gravity that is communicated via the work. As Weil tells us, '[The geniuses] give us…something equivalent to the actual density of the real, that density which life offers us every day but which we are unable to grasp because we are amusing ourselves with lies' (SNL 162). The artistic genius is fully committed to revealing, and not obscuring

9. 'Christ the Savior' (Christ Pantocrator), *circa* 1260, Hilandar Monastery, reflecting the impersonal beauty Weil admired.

or enhancing, harsh reality. It is for this reason that his/her personality should be absent from the creation and the creative process. Weil's comment about attentiveness in mathematical studies is instructive here: 'If a child is doing a sum and does it wrong, the mistake bears the stamp of his personality. If he does the sum exactly right, his personality does not enter into it at all' (ANTH 55). Instead, the attentive student or artist opens themselves to the truth of the world and is comfortable waiting for such revelation. The pen is poised right above the paper while awaiting the necessary and essential words—nothing more and nothing less. The primary activity of the attentive artist is one of negative effort: to reject what is inadequate, inessential, and unreal; the result will be nothing short of real beauty.

The precarious in nature

While the same basic principles of beauty in the realm of art apply to the beauty of the natural world, Weil emphasizes another set of characteristics in describing what she calls 'the order and beauty of the world': chance, precarity, and vulnerability. When she tells us that 'the presence of beauty in the world is the experimental proof of the possibility of incarnation', she means that there is a spark of the presence of the absolute or God in nature (FLN 83). But contrary to the idea of God as an omnipotent, static, and complete being, such incarnation in the natural world indicates a different sort of divine appearance: one that is fragile, precarious, humble, and suffering at times.

To say that the world is beautiful in Weilian terms means accepting the reality of the universe as a whole (not just our limited or preferred slice of it) as well as acknowledging the impersonal character of nature: the sun shines and the rain falls on the just and the unjust alike; natural disasters befall the relatively innocent and beautiful sunsets enthrall those who are vicious. 'Nothing less than the universe is beautiful', Weil writes (WG 112). Such a recognition entails a detached, stoical attitude that does not denigrate the world with its seeming randomness or overly sentimentalize it when we find it enjoyable. At the same time, the elements, plants, and animals of this world are transitory and vulnerable, here only by chance. Weil reflects:

The beings whom I love are creatures. They were born of a chance meeting between their father and mother. My meeting them is also a matter of chance. They will die.... To know things and beings that are limited as limited, with all one's soul, and to feel an infinite love for them—that is really leaving an open passage in oneself for contact between God and creation.   (N 483)

This character of chance is crucial in understanding beauty, for it shows us the extent to which we must *take care* of creation, not in spite of its fragility but because of it.

Weil frequently cites St Francis of Assisi as the exemplar of such care of the world and one who demonstrates how central the beauty of nature can be in Christian thought (Figure 10). She thought that his entire life was 'perfect poetry in action', as indicated, in part, by his choice of places for his solitary retreats or the sites for his convents. Moreover, she admired the way in which he lived in poverty, having stripped himself of everything in order to make communion with and take delight in the beauty of the world. This decreative orientation is the appropriate one for appreciating the world's beauty without our projections or interferences or sense of false divinity. For Weil it seemed that the closer to nothing a person could become, the more beauty would become apparent in the world and the more universal our perspective. She writes:

> I do not in the least desire that I should no longer be able to feel this created world, but that it should not be to me personally that it is made sensible. To me it cannot confide its secret, which is too lofty. But if only I go away, then creation and Creator will be able to exchange their secrets.
>
> ...The beauty of a landscape just at the moment when nobody is looking at it, absolutely nobody...To see a landscape such as it is when I am not there. When I am anywhere, I pollute the silence of earth and sky with my breathing and the beating of my heart.
>
> (N 422–3)

10. *St Francis Preaching to the Birds* by Giotto di Bondone.

There is a pragmatic angle to this aspiration for disappearance in nature; we know, for instance, that the smaller, the quieter, and the more still we make ourselves in the wild, the more likely it is that animals will behave naturally, come closer, and reveal their unknown and remarkable worlds. More broadly, our polluting practices, toxic inventions, and the resulting environmental catastrophes could be mitigated or even eliminated in some cases if we embraced Weil's decreative posture in the world. Giving up our imaginary position at the centre of the universe, listening and watching with reverent awe, we allow the beauty of the natural world to manifest more fully.

Outside of St Francis and a few others like St John of the Cross, Weil critiques the Christian tradition for having cut itself off from a love of the beauty of the world, condemning itself to a largely abstract and otherworldly existence, contrary to its esteem of divine incarnation. She found this strange and wondered how Christianity could 'call itself catholic' with this neglect of the universe itself. The Christian tradition, she wrote, could improve by embracing the 'Stoic's idea of filial piety for the city of the world' (WG 112). If we are attentive to nature, we find a sense of utter vulnerability and chance, which is a mark of existence and therefore of beauty. To love something while acknowledging its inevitable decline and death is to come to terms with our own mortality, too; it is to make peace with the void at the heart of creation.

Embodying stillness and silence before the natural world, or indeed before anything we desire and find beautiful, is analogous to prayer, Weil suggests. It is the height of attentiveness. In fact, this sort of self-renunciation and restraint is paradoxically the means to direct encounter with God, as opposed to our usual active searches, assertions of ideas, and grasping onto pleasing elements with which we wish to identify. 'Distance', she reflects, 'is the soul of beauty' (N 615).

Beholding at a distance

In Weil's *Notebooks*, we find: 'Beauty. A fruit one contemplates without stretching out one's hand' (N 283). The biblical story of Eve in the Garden of Eden is in the background of this unusual description of beauty. As we have seen, Weil frequently invokes Eve as a negative example of the ideal aesthetic-ethical orientation. She charges Eve with eating what she should have only beheld; Eve was too hasty and consumptive in her desire for the forbidden fruit. Her mistake, as Weil explained, was in appropriating and eating the fruit—not so much because God forbade it, as in the traditional recounting of the story, but because it represented a proprietary approach to a thing of beauty, something we should simply behold from a distance.

Yet to have a desire for something is to want to *have* that thing. In this sense, desire sets up an impossibility: as the ancient Greeks understand the meaning of desire, or *eros*, as soon as we possess the object of our desire, we no longer want it, by definition. Desire (as *eros*) is understood as the grasping space or distance between a state of lack and the resource or object that would fill that lacking. Weil's aesthetic philosophy is heavily influenced by this ancient Greek understanding of desire as the gap between an impoverished lover and the beloved (object or person) who could answer that desire. Like Plato, she believed that there is immense value in the love/desire itself, but the question is always where the love is directed. As we have seen, there is one legitimate 'object' of desire for Weil, and that is God or the good—even though the metaxu here on earth can be directly loved since they represent the incarnation of God.

Following Plato, Weil contends that true beauty can reorient us by transforming our base desires into noble desires for the good, and this transformation will effect a contemplative attitude in us. In particular, the attraction we have towards pure beauty is joined with a refusal to overtake and consume it:

> A thing that we perceive as beautiful is a thing which we do not touch, which we do not want to touch, for fear of damaging it. The energy supplied by other objects of desire can only be transmuted into spiritually usable energy through an act of detachment or

> refusal—declining the decoration or giving away the money. But the
> attraction of beauty already in itself implies a refusal. One is both
> attracted and kept at a distance. (SNL 124)

In short, what is beautiful instils a reverence in the attentive
subject that means keeping one's distance for fear of damaging or
polluting the purity of what is loved. Beauty confers respect.

For Weil, it is imperative, then, that we fasten onto this sort of
attraction, for it is a direct acknowledgement of our inner void
and our need for the good, and it results in a disposition that
recognizes the beauty, integrity, and sacredness of what is external
to us, beyond our particular interest in it. One central question is
whether we are actually able to recognize glimpses of absolute
beauty in the things and beings we desire. If we do not see beauty
piercing through what we love (or for Plato, if our soul has
forgotten the ultimate form of beauty), then there is nothing to
hold us back in our quest to consume; we see only opportunities
for our own gratification. While Plato offered the theory of
recollection as the explanation for human learning, growth of
wisdom, and recognition of beauty in particular individuals, Weil
translated this idea into her notion of attention. She illustrated
the phenomenon this way:

> Suppose I have had a thought and have forgotten it two hours
> later...I direct my attention for a few minutes towards an empty
> space; empty but real. Then suddenly the thought is there, beyond
> all possible doubt. I did not know what it was, and yet now
> I recognize it as being what I was waiting for. An everyday
> experience, and an unfathomable mystery. (SNL 121)

In such epiphanic moments, beauty composes us ethically. To
discover something beautiful and therefore worthy of love is to
simply desire its existence independent of ourselves. When we
encounter something truly beautiful, we simply desire that it
should be. A beautiful poem, for example, is one in which every

word, space, and punctuation feels absolutely necessary; the reader would not wish it any other way.

Beauty, for Weil, is God's lure and play. It has no purpose beyond helping us to lose ourselves for the sake of deeper levels of attention, in which we can sense the minutest details that normally get passed over. Although there is joy to be found in the discovery of these particulars, the greater significance of this aesthetic attention resides in the revelation of both limitation and mystery in the universe, which we encounter in our blessed metaxu. The greatest human masterpieces show us the truth of the human condition in relation to our desire for the transcendent, just out of reach. The natural world with its terrifying and sublime beauty discloses the blind and impersonal character of necessity, as well as the element of chance, which pervades creation and reminds us of our place, never at the centre. Each instance of beauty attracts us through these epiphanies towards some inexpressible and incomprehensible beyond. The beautiful, that is, humbles us as it compels us to confront divine mystery.

Chapter 7
Weil in the present and future

Simone Weil's philosophic influence on a variety of thinkers, artists, and writers has continued to grow since her untimely death in 1943. But the significance of her work has also been magnified, arguably due to the issues with which we continue to contend across the world and which she had addressed throughout her essays, letters, and notebooks. Without doubt, how we read and receive a thinker is largely shaped by our present social-political circumstances; Weil is a philosopher whose character and writings are more relevant than ever in analysing our contemporary crises, many of which are extensions or different versions of the same problems she witnessed in her life. Whether we are discussing the injustices of mechanized warehouse labour, the rise of fascist movements, the gross social-economic inequalities perpetuated by the uber-wealthy, neocolonialism, the destruction of the natural world, the hollowing out of formal education, or the growth of collectivism in religious life, Weil has something to say to us.

This small volume was completed in a time in which the world has seen growing authoritarianism, cult mentalities, nationalism, rampant use of deadly force by individuals and institutions, rapidly escalating global environmental catastrophes, and deepening social-economic asymmetries, none of which are being sufficiently confronted by the leaders of the world's most powerful countries. These crises, I argue, find their roots in an admixture of late capitalist values tinged with nationalist-religious fervour alongside a sweeping (if unconscious) nihilism that prepares the path for tyrants, violence, and destruction of communities and the world at large. Weil diagnosed many of our present ills and identified their root causes, noting our resentment of necessary limits, our inattentiveness, our propensity towards self-centredness and void-filling, and the ways in which we create dangerously powerful idols by conferring absolute values onto what is merely relative and temporal.

It remains to be seen whether we will heed her critiques and diagnoses in a manner that will make the world more liveable, sustainable, and harmonious for all of us. One point seems indisputable, though: in taking Weil seriously, the way forward will not centre on more human innovation, entertainment, and expansion but will instead require deep attention and the resulting radical decreation she unceasingly prescribed.

Scholarly influence

Many highly regarded philosophers and writers of the late 20th and early 21st centuries have been impacted by Weil's prescient observations and social critiques, and some have even credited her for important epiphanies in their own thinking. While there are too many to detail here, I will mention four notable examples of substantive engagement with Weil's thought.

The late French philosopher Emmanuel Levinas was a critic of Weil, particularly of her uncharitable reading of the Tanakh and Judaism in general. Two of his essays highlight these critiques: 'Simone Weil against the Bible' (1952) and 'Loving the Torah More than God' (1955). Moreover, he was critical of her mystical orientation, which he interpreted as a desired union with God and therefore as an obstacle to and distraction from one's ethical responsibility for the other person whom we encounter in the present—even though Weil thought we can love God only through our love of persons and the world.

Writer-philosopher Iris Murdoch was heavily influenced by Weil's Christian-Platonic ideas of the Good, the void, and attention, notions which shaped Murdoch's own theories of the existence of a moral reality, the significance of love, and the need to orient away from the self and towards others in gestures of attention—particularly as evident in her *The Sovereignty of Good* (1970) and *Metaphysics as a Guide to Morals* (1992). She explicitly credits Weil for her concept of attention, defining it as 'a just and loving gaze directed upon an individual reality' which is the central characteristic of a moral agent. Weil's *Waiting for God*, she noted, was one of the three most influential philosophical works on her writing, the other two being Plato's *Symposium* and Kierkegaard's *Fear and Trembling*.

Author and activist Susan Sontag was also impacted by Weil's description of attention, arguing that 'the nature of moral judgements depends on our capacity for paying attention', as does the craft of beautiful writing. When asked what writers ought to do, Sontag had said, 'Love words, agonize over sentences. And pay attention to the world.' But she also noted how Weil's moral authority is tied (as it is with others like Kierkegaard, Dostoevsky, Kafka, and Rimbaud) to suffering and 'unhealthiness'. Sontag surmised that many are attracted to Weil's extreme ideas because they do seem to be borne out of serious conviction, even if her readers have no interest in sharing her self-denying life or demanding ideals:

> I am thinking of the fanatical asceticism of Simone Weil's life, her contempt for pleasure and for happiness, her noble and ridiculous political gestures, her elaborate self-denials, her tireless courting of affliction; and I do not exclude her homeliness, her physical clumsiness, her migraines, her tuberculosis. No one who loves life would wish to imitate her dedication to martyrdom nor would wish

it for his children nor for anyone else whom he loves. Yet so far as we love seriousness, as well as life, we are moved by it, nourished by it. (Sontag 1963)

Sontag understood that we do not admire a figure like Weil because we agree with her; we admire her because of the honesty with which she articulated her ideas on paper and through her living, because her thought and her life were inextricable from one another.

Finally, Canadian classicist and poet Anne Carson has invoked Weil in her works, including *Eros: The Bittersweet* (1986) and *Decreation* (2005), the latter clearly indebted to the Weilian concept by the same name. Along with making use of her notions of love, detachment, and decreation, Carson delves into the spiritual aspects of Weil's biography, examining some of her most challenging practices, such as how Weil sought to 'undo the creature' within her with the physical manifestations of decreation. Alongside Weil, Carson draws parallels to other notable women—like Sappho, Marguerite Porete, and Annie Dillard—who problematize consumption, seek closeness to the divine, and understand suffering as a means to move beyond the self.

Levinas, Murdoch, Sontag, and Carson are but a very small sample of prominent thinkers who have been influenced by Weil's life and ideas. Some of these others include philosophers like Albert Camus, Giorgio Agamben, Maurice Blanchot, Georges Bataille, and Cornel West; and writers and journalists such as André Gide, T. S. Eliot, Flannery O'Connor, Elaine Scarry, Czesław Miłosz, and Chris Hedges. Weil's impact on young and emerging scholars continues to grow, too, as do the number of articles, books, and plays written about her ideas—no doubt a reflection of the fact that we continue to encounter many of the same social, political, and moral challenges that she keenly laid bare and sought to address during her own life.

Attending to our world today

At the time of writing, according to Oxfam, the world's 10 richest men possess more wealth than the bottom 40 per cent of humanity, or 3.1 billion people combined. At the same time, the International Institute for Democracy and Electoral Assistance reports that the world is witnessing 'a new low for global democracy'; more than a third of the world's population lives under authoritarian rule, while just 6.4% enjoy a 'full democracy'. Additionally, half of democratic governments are experiencing an erosion of their democracy, including the United States. While American and other democracies are in decline, a sense of political impotence has grown that has exacerbated anxieties and fuelled violence. For instance, one in five adults (50 million people) in the US believe that political violence is justified in at least some circumstances. Many religious adherents have actively contributed to this social disintegration; American Christian evangelicals, in particular, have made a power-centric, capitalist-imperialist vision of holiness their brand, centred around self-interested and profiteering demagogues.

The 'prosperity gospel' is perhaps the most recognizable ideology promoting the conflation of religious (in particular, American Protestant Christian) faith with material/financial success as well as good health. The prosperity gospel is not a new phenomenon; it can be traced back at least to the Pentecostal revivals of the post-Second World War years, reaching its maturity in the late 1970s through televangelists, new ministries, publications, and other national media. It made material success the measure of the strength of immaterial faith; where the former is lacking (say, with a low income or job loss), the cause is believed to be the person's faltering, weak faith. To demonstrate that faith, adherents are often (ironically) asked to devote more of their limited income to their churches and church leadership. A 2006 *Times* poll found that 17 per cent of American Christians identify with the movement, while a full 61 per cent agree with the premise that 'God wants people to be prosperous'.

As many scholars and commentators have noted—like Harvey Cox in his important book *The Market as God* (2016)—following the Second World War, there has been such a valorization of capitalist values that our economy has been deified, while many of our religious sites and practices have rebranded themselves in the image of multinational corporations. Cox, an American theologian who was also a reader of Weil and who was prompted by a friend to peruse the business sections of newspapers to find out what goes on in the 'real world', was surprised to discover so many similarities between the two worlds: 'The lexicon of the Wall Street Journal and the business sections of Time and Newsweek turned out to bear a striking resemblance to Genesis, the Epistle to the Romans, and Saint Augustine's City of God', he wrote. In both contexts we can find 'myths of origin, legends of the fall, and doctrines of sin and redemption'. To put this phenomenon in Weil's terms, we have witnessed the confluence of 'the language of the market' and that of the 'nuptial chamber', or the religiously intimate language usually reserved for prayer and sacred rites. Such an admixture represents a dangerous cocktail for souls desperate for material resources and meaning: as Weil notes, 'any end whatever is like a stick to a drowning man' (N 546).

Arguably, anyone who attends any 'contemporary' Christian worship service today is likely to get at least a whiff of the corporate odour, whether in the means of selling the faith or proselytizing, in the concern for the market/congregant numbers, in the exaltation of dedication to the group through work and sacrifice, in the creation of psychological dependency upon the organization, or in the product being sold—often a feel-good token to motivate productivity and further submission. There could not be a greater contrast to Weil's conception of religiosity, which is characterized by its connection with reality and impersonal necessity such that it is experienced as infinitely demanding and void-affirming:

> How does one distinguish between what is imaginary and what is real in the spiritual domain? A definite choice must be made in favor of a real hell rather than of an imaginary paradise. (N 321)

So, too, in the glowing offices of late capitalist corporations, one cannot help but sense religious elements like the importance of communal/brand identity; the proliferation of 'creeds'; the traditions, honours, and initiation rites bestowed upon employees to cement their loyalty and fervour; the promises of ever-elusive rewards such that submission isn't felt as such; and the mysterious and perennially unavailable though somehow omnipresent and surveilling leaders who enjoy a cult-like status. We live in a time in which religious and corporate values have been almost entirely overlaid; the zenith of this confluence may well be the arrival of neoliberalism in the mid-20th century, which has championed endless 'opportunities' for personal development and ways to prove one's 'worthiness' that always depend upon self-exploitation. What gets normalized in this neoliberal disciple is an endless affirmation, or *I can*, undergirded by their desire for indefinite progress under the watchful gaze of the god-boss. But in this context, self-fulfilment becomes self-exploitation, and vice versa. There is never any *real* satisfaction; in our neoliberal world, every so-called 'benchmark' turns out to be a springboard for the next (imperative) level of accomplishment—hence the dedication of the masses depends upon the strength of the illusions of earthly paradise which they/we are fed.

In her own time, Weil wrote that 'the glossy surface' of her civilization hid 'a real intellectual decadence', with values that had been turned on their heads. She noted that 'the inversion of the relation between means and ends—an inversion which is to a certain extent the law of every oppressive society—here becomes total or nearly so, and extends to nearly everything'. Writing two years before the famous scene in Charlie Chaplin's comedic film *Modern Times* (1936), in which the Tramp is force-fed his lunch by the Billows Feeding Machine while standing on the assembly line, Weil continued:

> Machines do not run in order to enable men to live, but we resign ourselves to feeding men in order that they may serve the machines. Money does not provide a convenient method for exchanging products; it is the sale of goods which is a means for keeping money in circulation. (OL 111)

While, in recent decades, our cultural critics have been warning us of the effects of machines and technologies generally considered benign—from mass media transmission of disinformation and 'infotainment' propaganda, to widespread usage of artificial intelligence, to communications technologies rendering us increasingly isolated and illiterate—we are just beginning to realize how our most celebrated 'innovations' (like social media platforms) have enabled the rise of malevolent actors and authoritarians, as well as the demise of facility with language and the value of truth. 'Where irrational opinions hold the place of ideas', Weil wrote, 'force is all-powerful' (OL 119). When fame (including infamy) and witty rejoinders become more revered than actual experts with their painstakingly researched and nuanced findings, and when faith in democratic institutions wanes as a result of an ultra-powerful oligarchic class wielding divisive strategies to bolster their own narrow interests, then the path is cleared for a strongman who will offer up fantasies of unlimited riches and paternalistic concern for the masses. In reality, of course, such an authoritarian only expands his power by manipulating, exploiting, and further oppressing the people; and it is not love he has for them but contempt and fear.

An authoritarian is fearful because his power is so precarious and contingent upon lies. Yet a tyrant hubristically wishes to be like God in terms of power (not love), that is, alone and self-sufficient.

He does not grasp, however, that his principle of action (fear) will be self-defeating: his self-isolation culminates in the vanishing of a common world and the sense of increased threats. That is, with hubristic isolation comes the realization of impotence, and with this sense of impotence comes persistent fear of the power of others, and this fear, in turn, reinforces the tyrant's will to dominate and self-isolate.

In short, it is an endless vicious cycle that, when taken to its fullest extent, leads to attempts to 'arrest' people—through incapacitation, exile, prison, exclusion, silencing, rewriting history, or outright annihilation—so that any unforeseen, free, or spontaneous acts that might hinder the tyrant's unrestrained terror can be prevented. What the person governing by terror wants most is maximum predictability (from others), with complete licence for his/her own agenda. In fact, capricious, illogical, and unnecessary violence is key to ensuring a dominator's sovereignty. Weil noted this phenomenon as a semblance between Nazi Germany and ancient Rome: 'Hitler and his men do not love war; they love domination and dream of nothing but peace—a peace in which their will is supreme, of course. Ancient Rome did likewise' (SE 96). She went on to describe the tactic of arbitrary force:

> [The principle of universal dominion] requires that no one may be allowed to think that he can influence in any way the will of the people which claims dominion; it must be proved by examples that neither determination, nor arms, nor treaties, nor past services, nor submissiveness, nor prayers are of any avail. That is why the Romans exhausted themselves in an interminable war against a little town whose existence was no threat, and whose destruction was of no advantage to them. They could not afford to tolerate its freedom. (SE 112)

Fear is therefore the origin and effect of isolation. But fear can quickly become credulity, as the latter is an easier psychical state to maintain. Of the Romans, Weil writes that their 'spectators were terror-struck; and since terror makes the soul credulous, the very perfidy of the Romans had the effect of strengthening rather than weakening their neighbors' inclination to believe them. People are eager to believe whatever they very much hope is true' (SE 103).

This point (of which we can find numerous examples today) cannot be emphasized enough: social-political disintegration grows because people are willing and eager to delude themselves about situations that incrementally destroy the foundation of their very existence, for the sake of the pleasantness of a belief, or for perceived loyalty, or a desire to align with power and force. And people will heed force-filled propaganda because theirs is a state of lonely anxiety which they escape by becoming addicted to an ersatz divinity or ideology which promises the world. This kind of adoration is contagious insofar as it seems to offer an instant community. But as we have seen, for Weil there is something irresistibly intoxicating and deceptive about the collective, given its alliance with prestige.

Have we, in our industrialized religio-capitalistic societies, made ourselves immune to the void and to the hunger that signals it? Certainly, now we have more and easier access to superficial distractions and false foods, as it were, than ever before. We have perhaps descended into a vortex of sensing entitlement not-to-suffer, of not-to-feel-hunger. Instead of looking at the beautiful, we have taken up the consumptive posture of voyeuristic watching of spectacles. This latter activity is not characterized by openness, for we go into watching with expectations, usually expectations of entertainment and anaesthetization. It is also an activity that protects power and privilege on one side, while, on the other side, certain groups of people are subjected to illusory fabrications at the hands of those who fashion these distractions.

In the urgency of our avoidance of truth, in our lust for control and power, we have become the personification of one end only of the metaphorical sword, that of brute violence and aggression:

> Contact with the sword causes the same defilement, whether it be through the handle or the point. For him who loves, its metallic coldness will not destroy love, but will give the impression of being abandoned by God. Supernatural love has no contact with force, but at the same time it does not protect the soul against the coldness of force, the coldness of steel.... If we want to have a love which will protect the soul from wounds, we must love something other than God. (N 497)

Being attentive to the world, according to Weil, means that we release the handle of the destructive sword and give up both comforting illusions and force. Clearly, this renunciation is risk filled. Letting the sword go may mean that we find ourselves quickly at its point. Modern psychology might call this move masochistic. But Weil tells us, 'This is not any kind of masochism. What excites masochists is only the *semblance* of cruelty, because they don't know what cruelty is' (FLN 260). Conversely, the one who attends to reality knows affliction and the absence of God, this other side of cruelty and power. It is in this tangible absence of the good that Weil says we must be vigilant in our love. Haste and distractions are, in this state, perpetual temptations. However, as Weil warned, 'alas for her if she gets tired and goes away. For the two places where God and humanity are waiting are at the same point in the fourth dimension...' (FLN 141).

What Simone Weil offers to the 21st century and beyond, I think, is a framework of 'the fourth dimension'—that is, a radical framework—from which to view social, cultural, political, and moral problems, a framework that challenges even our most progressive ethical theories. Hers is a paradigm for our present and future that centres on unapologetic truthfulness and self-decentring love of the world. In an age in which capitalism has subsumed all other values, in which political dishonesty and cynicism are the norm, in which sadism and shamelessness are glorified as cheap entertainment, and in which authoritarian violence is rationalized as patriotism, Weil's remarkable life and philosophy still calls us to look unflinchingly at this world in crisis and to remember our ever-present hunger for the good.

References

Chapter 1: A life and death of attention

De Beauvoir, Simone (1959), *Memoirs of a Dutiful Daughter*, trans. James Kirkup (New York: Harper & Row).

Du Plessix Gray, Francine (2001), *Simone Weil* (London: Penguin Books).

Fiedler, Leslie (2001), 'Introduction', *Waiting for God*, by Simone Weil (New York: Perennial Classics).

Fiori, Gabriella (1989), *Simone Weil: An Intellectual Biography*, trans. Joseph R. Berrigan (Athens, Ga.: University of Georgia Press). [For quotations about Weil's education and philosophical influences.]

Pétrement, Simone (1976), *Simone Weil: A Life*, trans. Raymond Rosenthal (New York: Pantheon Books). [For quotations about Weil's family life.]

Weil, Simone (1965), *Seventy Letters*, trans. Richard Rees (London: Oxford University Press).

Weil, Simone (2001), *Waiting for God*, trans. Emma Craufurd (New York: Perennial Classics).

Weil, Sylvie (2010), *At Home with André and Simone Weil*, trans. Benjamin Ivry (Evanston, Ill.: Northwestern University Press).

Chapter 2: Greek inspiration

Carson, Anne (2000), *Eros the Bittersweet* (Funks Grove, Ill.: Dalkey Archive Press).

Weil, Simone (1957), *Intimations of Christianity Among the Ancient Greeks* (New York: Routledge).

Weil, Simone (1968), *On Science, Necessity, and the Love of God*, trans. Richard Rees (London: Oxford University Press).

Weil, Simone (1970), *First and Last Notebooks*, trans. Richard Rees (London: Oxford University Press).

Weil, Simone (1986), 'The *Iliad* or the Poem of Force' and 'Human Personality', in *Simone Weil: An Anthology*, ed. Siân Miles (New York: Grove Press).

Weil, Simone (2001), *Waiting for God*, trans. Emma Craufurd (New York: Perennial Classics).

Weil, Simone (2004), *Notebooks*, trans. Arthur Wills (New York: Routledge).

Chapter 3: Labour and politics

Rabinbach, Anson (1992), *The Human Motor: Energy, Fatigue, and the Origins of Modernity* (Berkeley: University of California Press). [For quotations about Taylorism.]

Weil, Simone (1970), *First and Last Notebooks*, trans. Richard Rees (London: Oxford University Press).

Weil, Simone (1973), *Oppression and Liberty*, trans. Arthur Wills and John Petrie (Amherst, Mass.: University of Massachusetts Press).

Weil, Simone (1988), *Formative Writings: 1929–1941*, trans. Dorothy Tuck McFarland and Wilhelmina Van Ness (Amherst, Mass.: University of Massachusetts Press).

Weil, Simone (2001), *Waiting for God*, trans. Emma Craufurd (New York: Perennial Classics).

Weil, Simone (2002), *The Need for Roots*, trans. Arthur Wills (New York: Routledge).

Weil, Simone (2013), *On the Abolition of All Political Parties*, trans. Simon Leys (New York: New York Review Books).

Weil, Simone (2015), 'The First Condition for the Work of a Free Person', in *Simone Weil: Late Philosophical Writings*, trans. Lawrence Schmidt (Notre Dame: University of Notre Dame Press).

Chapter 4: Religion

Weil, Simone (2001), *Waiting for God*, trans. Emma Craufurd (New York: Perennial Classics).

Weil, Simone (2003), *Letter to a Priest* (London: Penguin Books).

Weil, Simone (2004), *Gravity and Grace*, trans. Emma Crawfurd and Mario von der Ruhr (New York: Routledge).

Weil, Simone (2004), *Notebooks*, trans. Arthur Wills (New York: Routledge).

Chapter 5: Ethics

Weil, Simone (1965), *Seventy Letters*, trans. Richard Rees (London: Oxford University Press).

Weil, Simone (1968), *On Science, Necessity, and the Love of God* (London: Oxford University Press).

Weil, Simone (1998), *Simone Weil: Selected Writings*, ed. Eric O. Springsted (Maryknoll, NY: Orbis Books).

Weil, Simone (2001), *Waiting for God*, trans. Emma Craufurd (New York: Perennial Classics).

Weil, Simone (2004), *Notebooks*, trans. Arthur Wills (New York: Routledge).

Weil, Simone (2004), *Gravity and Grace*, trans. Emma Crawfurd and Mario von der Ruhr (New York: Routledge).

Chapter 6: Beauty

Kearney, Richard (1988), *The Wake of Imagination* (New York: Routledge).

Weil, Simone (1968), *On Science, Necessity, and the Love of God* (London: Oxford University Press).

Weil, Simone (1970), *First and Last Notebooks*, trans. Richard Rees (London: Oxford University Press).

Weil, Simone (1978), *Lectures on Philosophy* (Cambridge: Cambridge University Press).

Weil, Simone (1986), *Simone Weil: An Anthology*, ed. Siân Miles (New York: Grove Press).

Weil, Simone (2001), *Waiting for God*, trans. Emma Craufurd (New York: Perennial Classics).

Weil, Simone (2004), *Notebooks*, trans. Arthur Wills (New York: Routledge).

Weil, Simone (2004), *Gravity and Grace*, trans. Emma Crawfurd and Mario von der Ruhr (New York: Routledge).

Chapter 7: Weil in the present and future

Burton, Tara Isabella (2017), 'The Prosperity Gospel, Explained', *Vox*, accessed here: <https://www.vox.com/identities/2017/9/1/

15951874/prosperity-gospel-explained-why-joel-osteen-believes-prayer-can-make-you-rich-trump>.

Carson, Anne (1986), *Eros the Bittersweet* (Princeton: Princeton University Press).

Carson, Anne (2006), *Decreation* (New York: Vintage Books).

Cox, Harvey (1999), 'The Market as God: Living in the New Dispensation', *The Atlantic*, accessed here: <https://www.theatlantic.com/magazine/archive/1999/03/the-market-as-god/306397/>.

Cox, Harvey (2016), *The Market as God* (Cambridge, Mass.: Harvard University Press).

International IDEA (2022), 'The Global State of Democracy 2022', accessed here: <https://www.idea.int/news-media/news/global-democracy-weakens-2022>.

Levinas, Emmanuel (1990), *Difficult Freedom: Essays on Judaism*, trans. Seán Hand (Baltimore: Johns Hopkins University Press).

Murdoch, Iris (1970), *The Sovereignty of Good* (New York: Routledge).

Murdoch, Iris (1992), *Metaphysics as a Guide to Morals* (London: Penguin Books).

Oxfam International (2022), '10 Richest Men Double Their Fortunes in Pandemic While Incomes of 99 Percent of Humanity Fall', accessed here: <https://www.oxfam.org/en/press-releases/ten-richest-men-double-their-fortunes-pandemic-while-incomes-99-percent-humanity>.

Pilkington, Ed (2022), 'One in Five U.S. Adults Condone "Justified" Political Violence, Mega Survey Finds', *The Guardian* (online), accessed here: <https://www.theguardian.com/us-news/2022/jul/19/one-in-five-us-adults-condone-political-violence-survey>.

Sontag, Susan (1963), 'Simone Weil', *The New York Review*, accessed here: <https://www.nybooks.com/articles/1963/02/01/simone-weil/>.

Weil, Simone (1970), *First and Last Notebooks*, trans. Richard Rees (London: Oxford University Press).

Weil, Simone (1973), *Oppression and Liberty*, trans. Arthur Wills and John Petrie (Amherst, Mass.: University of Massachusetts Press).

Weil, Simone (2004), *Notebooks*, trans. Arthur Wills (New York: Routledge).

Weil, Simone (2015), *Simone Weil: Selected Essays 1934–43*, ed. and trans. Richard Rees (Eugene, Ore.: Wipf & Stock).

Further reading

Listed below is a selection of recommended secondary works in English on Simone Weil's thought, corresponding to the themes within each chapter. Anyone interested in Weil should, however, begin with her own writings, particularly: *Waiting for God*, *Oppression and Liberty*, *The* Iliad *or the Poem of Force*, *First and Last Notebooks*, *The Notebooks of Simone Weil*, and *Simone Weil: Late Philosophical Writings* (translated by Eric O. Springsted and Lawrence E. Schmidt). There are some edited collections of her writings that, while decontextualizing some of her thought, nevertheless provide useful and accessible introductions to some of her core ideas, including: *Simone Weil: An Anthology* (edited by Siân Miles) and *Gravity and Grace* (translated by Emma Crawfurd and Mario von der Ruhr).

The latter, *Gravity and Grace*, is often treated as Weil's own work, and in some sense it is, since its contents are various selections drawn from her vast notebooks. However, Weil's friend Gustave Thibon had compiled the work following Weil's death and published it in 1947, providing the chapter/subject headings, culling fragments and statements from the notebooks to fit his subject headings, and therefore structuring her thought in a format that Weil had not done herself. In a way, then, this is Thibon's book, although the words are Weil's. Two consecutive statements in *Gravity and Grace* may appear as though they belong together but may, in fact, be separated by hundreds of pages in her notebooks, reflecting years of difference in her thought and philosophical evolution. Fortunately, Eric O. Springsted, with the assistance of notes from the late Martin Andic, has compiled a useful resource for locating quotations in *Gravity and Grace* in their original notebooks location. The key can be found here: <http://americanweilsociety.org/bibliography>

Still, *Gravity and Grace* can be incredibly helpful as a starting point for coming to know Weil. It remains helpful to me, as locating some of her quotations on a particular theme can be highly difficult to do in the massive and unorganized notebooks—which were like her workbooks. I have taken the liberty of quoting from *Gravity and Grace* on a few occasions in this volume, especially where I believed a succession of statements in Thibon's arrangement did concisely capture a concept of Weil's which was being explicated.

Chapter 1: A life and death of attention

Du Plessix Gray, Francine (2001), *Simone Weil* (London: Penguin Books).

Fiori, Gabriella (1989), *Simone Weil: An Intellectual Biography*, trans. Joseph R. Berrigan (Athens, Ga.: University of Georgia Press).

Perrin, J. M. and Gustave Thibon (2003), *Simone Weil as We Knew Her* (New York: Routledge).

Pétrement, Simone (1976), *Simone Weil: A Life*, trans. Raymond Rosenthal (New York: Pantheon Books).

Von der Ruhr, Mario (2006), *Simone Weil: An Apprenticeship in Attention* (London: Continuum Books).

Weil, Sylvie (2010), *At Home with André and Simone Weil*, trans. Benjamin Ivry (Evanston, Ill.: Northwestern University Press).

Chapter 2: Greek inspiration

Doering, E. Jane and Eric O. Springsted (2004), *The Christian Platonism of Simone Weil* (Notre Dame: University of Notre Dame Press).

Springsted, Eric O. (1983), *Christus Mediator: Platonic Mediation in the Thought of Simone Weil* (Chico, Calif.: Scholars Press).

Chapter 3: Labour and politics

Avery, Desmond (2008), *Beyond Power: Simone Weil and the Notion of Authority* (New York: Lexington Books).

Bourgault, Sophie and Julie Daigle, eds (2020), *Simone Weil, Beyond Ideology?* (Cham: Palgrave Macmillan).

Davis, Benjamin P. (2023), *Simone Weil's Political Philosophy: Field Notes from the Margins* (Lanham, Md: Rowman and Littlefield).

Doering, E. Jane (2010), *Simone Weil and the Specter of Self-Perpetuating Force* (Notre Dame, Ind.: University of Notre Dame Press).

Von der Ruhr, Mario (2006), *Simone Weil: An Apprenticeship in Attention* (New York: Continuum).

Chapter 4: Religion

Bingemer, Maria Clara (2015), *Simone Weil: Mystic of Passion and Compassion*, trans. Karen M. Kraft (Eugene, Ore.: Cascade Books).

McCullough, Lissa (2014), *The Religious Philosophy of Simone Weil* (London: I. B. Tauris).

Rozelle-Stone, A. Rebecca and Lucian Stone (2013), *Simone Weil and Theology* (London: Bloomsbury T&T Clark).

Springsted, Eric O. (1986), *Simone Weil and the Suffering of Love* (Cambridge, Mass.: Cowley).

Vetö, Miklos (1994), *The Religious Metaphysics of Simone Weil*, trans. Joan Dargan (Albany, NY: State University of New York Press).

Chapter 5: Ethics

Cha, Yoon Sook (2017), *Decreation and the Ethical Bind: Simone Weil and the Claim of the Other* (New York: Fordham University Press).

Davis, Benjamin P. and Rebecca Rozelle-Stone (2021), 'Simone Weil', *Stanford Encyclopedia of Philosophy*: <https://plato.stanford.edu/entries/simone-weil/>

Rozelle-Stone, Rebecca, ed. (2017), *Simone Weil and Continental Philosophy* (London: Rowman and Littlefield, International).

Chapter 6: Beauty

Bell, Richard H. (1993), *Simone Weil's Philosophy of Culture* (Cambridge: Cambridge University Press).

Dargan, Joan (1999), *Simone Weil: Thinking Poetically* (Albany, NY: State University of New York Press).

Dunaway, John M. and Eric O. Springsted, eds (1996), *The Beauty that Saves: Essays on Aesthetics and Language in Simone Weil* (Macon, Ga.: Mercer University Press).

Pick, Anat (2011), *Creaturely Poetics: Animality and Vulnerability in Literature and Film* (New York: Columbia University Press).

Chapter 7: Weil in the present and future

Rozelle-Stone, A. Rebecca and Lucian Stone, eds (2010), *The Relevance of the Radical: Simone Weil 100 Years Later* (London: Continuum Books).

Springsted, Eric O. (2021), *Simone Weil for the Twenty-first Century* (Notre Dame, Ind.: University of Notre Dame Press).

Zaretsky, Robert (2021), *The Subversive Simone Weil: A Life in Five Ideas* (Chicago: University of Chicago Press).

Index

For the benefit of digital users, indexed terms that span two pages
(e.g., 52–53) may, on occasion, appear on only one of those pages.

Simone Weil

CITIZENSHIP
A Very Short Introduction
Richard Bellamy

Interest in citizenship has never been higher. But what does it mean to be a citizen of a modern, complex community? Why is citizenship important? Can we create citizenship, and can we test for it? In this fascinating Very Short Introduction, Richard Bellamy explores the answers to these questions and more in a clear and accessible way. He approaches the subject from a political perspective, to address the complexities behind the major topical issues. Discussing the main models of citizenship, exploring how ideas of citizenship have changed through time from ancient Greece to the present, and examining notions of rights and democracy, he reveals the irreducibly political nature of citizenship today.

'Citizenship is a vast subject for a short introduction, but Richard Bellamy has risen to the challenge with aplomb.'

Mark Garnett, TLS

COMMUNISM
A Very Short Introduction
Leslie Holmes

The collapse of communism was one of the most defining moments of the twentieth century. At its peak, more than a third of the world's population had lived under communist power. What is communism? Where did the idea come from and what attracted people to it? What is the future for communism? This Very Short Introduction considers these questions and more in the search to explore and understand communism. Explaining the theory behind its ideology, and examining the history and mindset behind its political, economic and social structures, Leslie Holmes examines the highs and lows of communist power and its future in today's world.

Very readable and with its wealth of detail a most valuable reference book.

Gwyn Griffiths, Morning Star

www.oup.com/vsi

CRITICAL THEORY
A Very Short Introduction
Stephen Eric Bronner

In its essence, Critical Theory is Western Marxist thought with the emphasis moved from the liberation of the working class to broader issues of individual agency. Critical Theory emerged in the 1920s from the work of the Frankfurt School, the circle of German-Jewish academics who sought to diagnose--and, if at all possible, cure--the ills of society, particularly fascism and capitalism. In this book, Stephen Eric Bronner provides sketches of famous and less famous representatives of the critical tradition (such as George Lukács and Ernst Bloch, Theodor Adorno and Walter Benjamin, Herbert Marcuse and Jurgen Habermas) as well as many of its seminal texts and empirical investigations.

www.oup.com/vsi

FRENCH LITERATURE
A Very Short Introduction
John D. Lyons

The heritage of literature in the French language is rich,
varied, and extensive in time and space; appealing both to its
immediate public, readers of French, and also to aglobal
audience reached through translations and film adaptations.
French Literature: A Very Short Introduction introduces this lively
literary world by focusing on texts - epics, novels, plays, poems,
and screenplays - that concern protagonists whose adventures
and conflicts reveal shifts in literary and social practices. From
the hero of the medieval *Song of Roland* to the Caribbean
heroines of *Tituba, Black Witch of Salem* or the European
expatriate in Japan in *Fear and Trembling*, these problematic
protagonists allow us to understand what interests writers and
readers across the wide world of French.

www.oup.com/vsi

KEYNES
A Very Short Introduction
Robert Skidelsky

John Maynard Keynes (1883–1946) is a central thinker of the twentieth century, not just an economic theorist and statesman, but also in economics, philosophy, politics, and culture. In this *Very Short Introduction* Lord Skidelsky, a renowned biographer of Keynes, explores his ethical and practical philosophy, his monetary thought, and provides an insight into his life and works. In the recent financial crisis Keynes's theories have become more timely than ever, and remain at the centre of political and economic discussion. With a look at his major works and his contribution to twentieth-century economic thought, Skidelsky considers Keynes's legacy on today's society.

PHILOSOPHY OF RELIGION

A Very Short Introduction

Tim Bayne

What is the philosophy of religion? How can we distinguish it from theology on the one hand and the psychology/sociology of religious belief on the other? What does it mean to describe God as 'eternal'? And should religious people want there to be good arguments for the existence of God, or is religious belief only authentic in the absence of these good arguments?

In this *Very Short Introduction* Tim Bayne introduces the field of philosophy of religion, and engages with some of the most burning questions that philosophers discuss. Considering how 'religion' should be defined, and whether we even need to be able to define it in order to engage in the philosophy of religion, he goes on to discuss whether the existence of God matters. Exploring the problem of evil, Bayne also debates the connection between faith and reason, and the related question of what role reason should play in religious contexts. Shedding light on the relationship between science and religion, Bayne finishes by considering the topics of reincarnation and the afterlife.

RUSSELL
A Very Short Introduction
A. C. Grayling

Bertrand Russell was one of the most famous and important philosophers of the twentieth century. In this account of his life and work A. C. Grayling introduces both Russell's contributions to logic and philosophy, and his wide-ranging views on education, politics, war, and sexual morality.

Russell is credited with being one of the founders of modern analytic philosophy, and also with playing an important part in the revolution in social attitudes witnessed throughout the world. This *Very Short Introduction* gives a clear survey of Russell's wide ranging philosophical achievements.

www.oup.com/vsi

THE FRENCH REVOLUTION

A Very Short Introduction

William Doyle

Beginning with a discussion of familiar images of the French Revolution, garnered from Dickens, Baroness Orczy, and Tolstoy, this *Very Short Introduction* leads the reader to the realization that we are still living with the legacy of the French Revolution. William Doyle shows how it destroyed age-old cultural, institutional, and social structures in France and beyond. Doyle then explains how the *ancien régime* became *ancien* and examines cases in which achievement failed to match ambition. To do so, he explores its consequences in the arenas of public affairs and responsible government, and ends with thoughts on why the revolution has been so controversial.

'A brilliant combination of narrative and analysis, this masterly essay provides the best introduction to its subject in any language.'

Tim Blanning, University of Cambridge

www.oup.com/vsi